AF705987

Social Security Law in Austria

Social Security Law in Austria

Second Edition

Nora Melzer

This book was originally published as a monograph in the International Encyclopaedia of Laws/Social Security Law.

Founding Editor: Roger Blanpain
General Editor: Frank Hendrickx
Volume Editor: Willy van Eeckhoutte

Wolters Kluwer

Published by:
Kluwer Law International B.V.
PO Box 316
2400 AH Alphen aan den Rijn
The Netherlands
E-mail: lrs-sales@wolterskluwer.com
Website: www.wolterskluwer.com/en/solutions/kluwerlawinternational

Sold and distributed by:
Wolters Kluwer Legal & Regulatory U.S.
920 Links Avenue
Landisville, PA 17538
United States of America
E-mail: customer.service@wolterskluwer.com

ISBN 978-94-035-4927-9

e-Book: ISBN 978-94-035-4937-8
web-PDF: ISBN 978-94-035-4947-7

The Author

Dr Nora Melzer is an Associate Professor at the Department of Labour Law and Law of Social Security at the University of Graz, Austria, and a Lecturer at the University of Klagenfurt, Austria, where she teaches Austrian and European Labour Law and the Law of Social Security and Anti-discrimination Law.

She has published books on the minimum wage tariff (*Mindestlohntarif*, an executive order by the Austrian Federal Conciliation Board) and teleworking, and commentaries on continued wage payment, works organization and selected collective agreements, and more than fifty articles, primarily in the fields of Austrian, European and international labour law and the law of social security. Finally, she is the Austrian contributor to the *International Labour Law Reports*.

The Author

Table of Contents

List of Abbreviations

AUVA	*Allgemeine Unfallversicherungsanstalt*
BGBl	*Bundesgesetzblatt*
BKK	*Betriebskrankenkasse*
BVA	*Versicherungsanstalt der öffentlich Bediensteten*
BVAEB	*Versicherungsanstalt öffentlich Bediensteter, Eisenbahnen und Bergbau*
ECJ	European Court of Justice
EEA	European Economic Area
GKK	*Gebietskrankenkassen*
idF	*in der Fassung* (Current Version)
ÖGK	*Österreichische Gesundheitskasse*
PVA	Pensionsversicherungsanstalt
RGBl	*Reichsgesetzblatt*
StGBl	*Staatsgesetzblatt*
SVA	*Sozialversicherungsanstalt der gewerblichen Wirtschaft*
SVB	*Sozialversicherungsanstalt der Bauern*
SVS	*Sozialversicherungsanstalt der Selbständigen*
VAEB	*Versicherungsanstalt für Eisenbahnen und Bergbau*

List of Abbreviations

General Introduction

1. Social law represents the sum of legal provisions governing benefits provided by the state to protect people in situations where they are not (or are no longer) able to provide for their own living expenses. The state organizes, finances and monitors social benefits. Such situations are referred to as social risks. The most significant social risks are: sickness, old age, the need for long-term care, unemployment, maternity, incapacity or reduced capacity to work, accidents at work and occupational diseases, family burdens, death of the family breadwinner and other involuntary loss of support.

Chapter 1. Historical Background

2. For a long time, the state did not take any action to provide care and assistance to people in need of help. These responsibilities were primarily organized by the church and its sub-organizations, such as various charitable orders, private individuals and guilds; however, the people concerned were not legally entitled to these services, and benefits were only provided to certain groups.

3. Changes only occurred towards the end of the nineteenth century. When introducing modern social security law, Austria based its policy primarily on the legislation of Bismarck in the 1880s. In 1888, the Workers' Accident Insurance Act and the Workers' Health Insurance Act were adopted (RGBl. Nr. 1/1888, RGBl. Nr. 33/1888). In 1906, the law on pension insurance for employees was passed (RGBl. Nr. 1/1907). At the beginning of the 1920s, during which comprehensive social reforms took place – especially within labour law – unemployment insurance was introduced (StGBl. Nr. 153/1920). In the late 1920s, a law on pension insurance for workers was also passed (BGBl. Nr. 125/1927). However, due to a 'prosperity clause', it was not implemented accordingly as the economic situation had been extremely bad. In 1939, in the course of the occupation of Austria by Germany, the German legal system, including the German Salaried Employees Insurance Act, was adopted.

4. After World War II, parts of these laws remained. On 1 January 1956, the General Social Insurance Act (BGBl. Nr. 189/1955) came into force, which essentially regulates social security for dependent employees. Further regulations followed to include all gainfully employed persons, in particular, the Commercial Social Security Act (BGBl. Nr. 560/1978) and the Farmers' Social Security Act (BGBl. Nr. 559/1978). In 1996 – Austria played a pioneering role – free employees were finally also given social security cover and have been subject to full insurance under the General Social Insurance Act ever since – just like dependent employees. In addition, further regulations were introduced in other areas, such as the insolvency pay protection in 1978 (Act on Safeguarding Employees' Claims in the Event of the Employer's Insolvency, BGBl. Nr. 324/1977) or provisions for long-term care for all in 1993 (Federal Care Allowance Act, BGBl. Nr. 110/1993). In 2001, the childcare allowance was introduced, a social benefit for parents, which is granted for a certain time after birth (BGBl. I Nr. 103/2001).

Chapter 2. Structures and Characteristics of the Austrian Social Security System

§1. Systematic Classification of Social Law

5. The present social law is divided into three major areas: social insurance, social welfare and social compensation. The differentiation is not only based on their financing, that is, whether they are financed through tax or contributions by the recipients, but also on the basis of the cause of the risk affecting the person concerned. Further aspects of differentiation concern the question of whether a recipient has a legal claim to receive social benefits or whether granting of the benefits is within the social security body's discretion.

I. Social Insurance

6. The term 'insurance' refers to a group of people who all potentially face specific risks and make contributions to a common fund to have sufficient financial back-up. Through these funds, the benefits which are granted to each person exposed to a social risk are financed by the whole community of insured persons and need not be paid by one person alone. Social insurance is a grouping of people ordered by law to provide financial security in the event of certain risks in life.

7. The Austrian social insurance system is closely linked to gainful employment and the establishment of a risk community according to professional groups, as well as the principle of compulsory insurance.

A. Establishing a Risk Community According to Professional Groups

8. Social security, organized according to the *Bismarck* system, is primarily linked to gainful employment and, subsequently, to a specific type of work. For this purpose, the social security laws group various categories of workers into risk communities (communities of insured persons), for instance, all employees or all farmers, whose occupational groups constitute each risk community has been developed historically. In some cases, an additional differentiation is made based on which life risks are covered by the respective community of insured persons (such as age or illness); based on this, a distinction is made between the different branches of insurance (such as pension insurance or health insurance). The legally defined members of the relevant risk community are obliged to make contributions, which are generally based on the level of their income; these contributions are used to fund support when a risk ('insured event') occurs. In this way, the risk of the individual is shifted to a group, here to the relevant risk community.

B. Compulsory Insurance

9. The community of insured persons' finances benefits their members in the event of an insured event. In order to guarantee financial assistance at all times, it is necessary to have appropriate financial coverage through the contributions of the members. In addition, in order to prevent the community of insured persons from rejecting certain future members if the likelihood of their risks is higher than those of others, the Austrian social security system follows the 'principle of statutory compulsory insurance' (*Prinzip der gesetzlichen Pflichtversicherung*).

10. All employed persons of a professional group who fulfil the legal criteria (such as having a trade licence or having an employment contract) automatically belong to the respective risk community and have to pay contributions. The membership of the risk community and the contribution are ordered by law. Only in a few areas is the insurance system organized according to the 'principle of the obligation to insure' (*Prinzip der Versicherungspflicht*); this applies, for instance, to certain freelancers. Such persons must also belong to a risk community, but they can choose the relevant insurance institution or insurance provider themselves.

11. The principle of statutory compulsory insurance applies to all other gainfully employed persons: if he or she fulfils the legal requirements, they are *ex lege* or *ipso iure* a member of the respective community of insured persons and can receive benefits from this insurance. This is also the case if a notification to the insurance body has not been made by the employer (*Meldeunabhängigkeit der Pflichtversicherung*); that is why even illicit workers can claim benefits in the case of illness regardless of the formal criteria. It has to be added that, however, there is a legal obligation to report, which means that disregarding the obligation to report leads to sanctions (like supplements to contributions, interest or fines) but, in principle, not to the loss or revocation of insurance benefits (for the limitation on the recognition of pension periods, *see* Part VIII Chapter 2).

C. Solidarity Ex Lege Insurance

12. The principle of compulsory insurance is supplemented by the principle of solidarity. The mandatory contributions which are laid down by law are not graded according to individual risk but are based solely on the individual's income (with a maximum limit). Consequently, all employees earning a certain amount pay the same contribution regardless of the number of co-insured family members or their health constitution. Furthermore, all employees get the same level of medical treatment – regardless of the size of their contributions. Such a solidarity-based approach enables insured people with many children, people with low incomes or elderly and sick people to benefit from the same insurance cover necessary for their well-being. If there were no such solidarity-based compulsory insurance, older people, people with many children, or those who are often ill would face considerably worse conditions since private insurance companies operate on a profit-oriented basis.

D. Contract Between Generations

13. The Austrian social security system has, so far, mainly been financed by contributions from the persons insured following the pay-as-you-go system. In this model, the contributions received are not saved in the long term or invested for each individual contributor but are immediately used to pay for services to other insured persons. In this way, all contributors help to finance the current pensions, relying on future generations to do the same. This approach is referred to as the contract between generations (*Generationenvertrag*).

II. Social Welfare

14. Benefits of social welfare are sometimes seen as the 'last social safety net' for persons in need of support who are not entitled to other benefits. This second field of social security is divided into general social assistance and the area of long-time nursing and care. Benefits of general social assistance include monthly cash benefits to secure living costs and housing needs, but there is also one-off assistance granted in emergencies (such as grants for funeral expenses) or assistance in achieving the ability to work. In addition, the recipients of social assistance are health-insured.

15. Both forms of social welfare are financed by tax revenues; welfare does not operate according to the insurance principle; however, it is required that the persons concerned are in an impecunious state. Beneficiaries are not required to have paid contributions. The main criterion for granting benefits is the need for assistance or social hardship of the recipient; in particular, the recipient is no longer able to cover their own subsistence or housing needs by themself or with the help of their relatives.

16. Moreover, social assistance is a subsidiary means of support through social security; it is only granted when there is no cover by social insurance or other state institutions. The conditions for benefits must be examined in each individual case. As a matter of principle, the potential benefit recipient must use his or her own means and efforts to earn a living.

III. Social Compensation Benefits for Victims and as a Reward

17. Social compensation, as the third part of Austrian social security, is divided into two types:

(1) Some benefits are granted as compensation as damages for extraordinary victims of measures of the state or comparable risks.
(2) Others are granted as a reward for exceptional services to the state or the common good.

18. Social compensation benefits are financed by tax revenue; beneficiaries need not have made contributions.

§2. Public Law Character of Social Security Benefits

19. The Austrian social security system is designed under public law; social security benefits are handled as part of an administrative procedure under public law. The insured person has a public right to the mandatory benefits (*Pflichtleistungen*) provided by law for the respective occupational group, as well as to the additional benefits provided by the statutes of the respective social insurance institutions. If such a claim is rejected, this must be done in the form of a decision, which can then be challenged by legal action (*see* General Introduction Chapter 3 §2 IV).

20. In addition to mandatory benefits, there are also voluntary benefits (*freiwillige Leistungen*), which must also be expressly designated as such by the respective legal provisions. Voluntary benefits are also granted as part of public administration. There is, however, no legal entitlement to receive these benefits; instead, they are granted at the free discretion of the social insurance institution (e.g., certain benefits of the health insurance in accordance with §154 section 1 General Social Insurance Act in case of an impairment).

Chapter 3. Sources of Social Security Law

21. In many countries – including Austria – social law and social protection are characterized by the principle of territoriality *(Territorialitätsprinzip)*. In the case of Austria, this means that – regardless of their citizenship – principally all employed persons working in Austria are subject to full insurance (§§3, 4 General Social Insurance Act). The Austrian compulsory insurance, therefore, ends if the provision of the service is solely owed abroad (§3 section 3 General Social Insurance Act). However, there are exceptions to this rule: the Austrian compulsory insurance system remains applicable to employees if their labour maintains a certain domestic reference *(Ausstrahlungsgrundsatz)*. An important example of this *principle of transference* is seconded employees (§3 section 2 General Social Insurance Act).

22. In order to create common international standards in the area of social security, to ensure better protection for employees and to prevent exploitation through cross-border work or of employees from emerging countries, several international and European agreements have been concluded, or corresponding regulations have been enacted.

§1. International and European Sources

I. International Organizations

A. International Labour Organization

23. The law of the International Labour Organization applicable under the Austrian social system is the Social Security (Minimum Standards) Convention, 1952 (No. 102) (BGBl. Nr. 33/1970).

II. European Organizations

A. The Council of Europe

24. The important regulations by the Council of Europe that are relevant to Austrian Social Security law are as follows:

(1) European Social Charter (BGBl. Nr. 460/1969 idF BGBl. Nr. 284/1970); European Social Charter revised (BGBl. Nr. 112/2011).
(2) European Convention on Human Rights (ECHR) (BGBl. Nr. 210/1958): The ECHR has been ratified in Austria even at constitutional level, which means that it is directly applicable and constitutes a review standard of the Austrian Constitutional Court.

B. The European Union

25. The most important regulations of the EU for Austrian Social Security law are as follows:

(1) Regulation (EC) No. 883/2004 of the European Parliament and of the Council of 29 April 2004 on the coordination of social security systems.
(2) Regulation (EC) No. 987/2009 of the European Parliament and of the Council of 16 September 2009 laying down the procedure for implementing Regulation (EC) No. 883/2004 on the coordination of social security systems.
(3) Article 7 section 2 Regulation (EU) No. 492/2011 of the European Parliament and of the Council of 5 April 2011 on freedom of movement for workers within the Union.
(4) Council Directive 79/7/EEC of 19 December 1978 on the progressive implementation of the principle of equal treatment for men and women in matters of social security.
(5) Directive 2006/54/EC of the European Parliament and of the Council of 5 July 2006 on the implementation of the principle of equal opportunities and equal treatment of men and women in matters of employment and occupation (recast).

C. National Unilateral and Multilateral Intergovernmental Agreements

26. Austria has – especially during the period before joining the EU – concluded separate agreements on social security with many individual states; in some cases, the parties to such agreements are even several states. Essential content of such agreements with one or more other states is the stipulation of equal treatment of the nationals of the contracting states in the area of social security, for example, the aggregation of insurance periods that have been completed in the respective contracting states.

27. Major examples of such individual treaties are Austria's agreements with Australia, Great Britain, Israel, the Philippines and the US. One example of a quadrilateral agreement is the agreement between Austria, Germany, Liechtenstein and Switzerland (*Agreement between the Federal Republic of Germany, the Principality of Liechtenstein, the Republic of Austria and the Swiss Confederation in the field of social security, including annexes and final protocol*, BGBl. Nr. 464/1980). Agreements with international organizations in the field of social security are, for instance, those with the IAEA (*Agreement between the International Atomic Energy Agency and the Republic of Austria regarding the headquarters of the International Atomic Energy Agency*, BGBl. Nr. 82/1958), the IOM (*Agreement between the Republic of Austria and the International Organization for Migration regarding the legal status of the organization in Austria and the headquarters of its offices in Vienna*, BGBl. III Nr. 115/2014) or the United Nations High Commissioner for Refugees (*Agreement between the Austrian Federal Government, hereinafter referred to as 'the Government', and the Office of the United Nations High Commissioner for Refugees, hereinafter referred to as 'UNHCR', concerning the cooperation of UNHCR in asylum procedures where the application has been filed at the time of the border control following entry via an airport*, BGBl. III Nr. 32/2003).

28. The above-mentioned agreements constitute national law. As special laws, they supersede principally contradictory Austrian provisions in this area; however, it is difficult to clarify the relationship of such individual agreements if they concern states which are also EU members. In principle, EU law would take precedence, but the individual agreements sometimes have a more extensive scope of application so that wider regulations would remain applicable. Some of the older individual agreements were, therefore, replaced by supplementary agreements. According to the European Court of Justice (ECJ), the agreements are applicable if they are more favourable and the employee has made use of the freedom of movement before the regulation came into force (ECJ C-227/89, *Ronfeldt*; ECJ C-475/93, *Thevenon*).

§2. National Sources

I. Constitutional Laws

29. In contrast to the area of 'labour law', the Austrian federal constitution does not contain an article on 'social law'; the division of social law into 'social insurance law' (*Sozialversicherungsrecht*), 'care' (*Versorgung*) and 'social assistance' (*Sozialhilfe*) is clearly evident. In general, the federal legislature is responsible; federalist elements in favour of the states are found primarily in enforcement and implementation.

A. Federal Competences in Legislation and Administration

30. In the area of social law, the federal government is responsible for both legislation and administration concerning social insurance as well as long-term care benefits and social compensation law (Article 10 section 1 No. 11 Federal Constitutional Law). Consequently, laws in the area of health insurance, pension insurance, accident insurance, unemployment insurance, as well as care allowance and social compensation of damages, are federal laws.

31. These matters are generally handled by the federal government, although in the areas of health insurance, pension insurance and accident insurance, the federal government is supported by special administrative bodies (the social insurance institutions), which are organized as self-governing bodies. The federal legislator is also responsible for their establishment.

B. Competencies Shared Between the Federal and State Governments

32. Social assistance does not fall – due to the lack of contributions by the recipients – within the scope of social insurance, which is regulated in Article 10 section 1 No. 11 Federal Constitutional Law; instead, there is a separate regulation under the outdated term 'the poor' (*Armenwesen*) in Article 12 section 1 No. 1 Federal Constitutional Law. According to this provision, the federal government is responsible for the basic legislation (*Grundsatzgesetzung*) and the federal states for the implementing legislation (*Ausführungsgesetzgebung*) and administration (*Verwaltung*). Thus, the Federation is given the responsibility to establish a uniform legal framework for regulations in this area, which may be specified to a certain extent by the states.

33. The federal government adopted the Federal Social Assistance Basic Law (BGBl. I Nr. 41/2019). It includes mainly cash and non-cash benefits regarding general subsistence and housing needs. In compliance with this general framework and as a supplement to these regulations at federal law, the states may provide other or additional social assistance benefits under their own legislation. That is why, there are very different regulations at state level.

II. Federal and State Laws and Statutes (Non-constitutional Level)

34. The General Social Insurance Act (*ASVG*, BGBl. Nr. 189/1955) regulates health insurance, pension insurance and accident insurance for dependent employees (employees and free employees). Furthermore, it also regulates accident insurance for commercial and freelance self-employed persons.

35. The Commercial Social Security Act (*GSVG*, BGBl. Nr. 560/1978) regulates health insurance and pension insurance for the self-employed, in particular, not only for those self-employed persons who work on the basis of a trade licence but also for the 'new' self-employed persons who are allowed to work without a trade licence (*see* General Introduction Chapter 4 §1 V).

36. The Farmers' Social Security Act (*BSVG*, BGBl. Nr. 559/1978) regulates health insurance, accident insurance and pension insurance for self-employed farmers and foresters.

37. The Liberal Professions Social Security Act (*FSVG*, BGBl. Nr. 624/1978) regulates health insurance and pension insurance for certain freelancers like physicians, architects, and pharmacists. The groups of notaries, however, have been given their own law; their social security is governed comprehensively by the Notary Insurance Law (*NVG* 2020, BGBl. I Nr. 128/2020).

38. The Civil Servants Health and Accident Insurance Law (*B-KUVG*, BGBl. Nr. 200/1967) regulates health insurance and accident insurance for federal contract staff and civil servants, university employees and public officials.

39. The Artists' Social Insurance Fund Act (*K-SVFG*, BGBl. I Nr. 131/2000) regulates the organization of the Artists' Fund as well as the conditions for a subsidy to cover their contributions to health, pension and accident insurance.

40. The Unemployment Insurance Act (*AlVG*, BGBl. Nr. 609/1977) covers unemployment insurance; the Federal Care Allowance Act (*BPGG*, BGBl. Nr. 110/1993) governs the requirements for the care allowance and the Childcare Allowance Act (*KBGG*, BGBl. I Nr. 103/2001) the childcare allowance.

41. The General Pensions Act (*APG*, BGBl. I Nr. 142/2004) harmonized the different pension systems to the so-termed new law of pension insurance (*see* Part VIII Chapter 1 §2).

III. Autonomous Legal Sources of National Social Security Institutions

42. Each individual social insurance institution (*Sozialversicherungsträger*), as well as the umbrella organization of all social insurance institutions (*Dachverband der Sozialversicherungsträger*), is a self-governing public body. In their own affairs, they may act without instructions. Nevertheless, they remain under supervision by the competent federal minister. For the fulfilment of their responsibilities, the law authorizes the social security institutions to issue general and individual sources of law with sovereign effect; moreover, they are authorized to conclude contracts under private law.

A. Statutes

43. The umbrella organization of social insurance institutions and each social insurance institution are authorized and obliged to issue a statute (*Satzung*, §§453 et seq. General Social Insurance Act). The statutes are regulations which must be published on the Internet and must be approved by the federal minister responsible. The umbrella association of social insurance institutions has adopted a model statute (*Mustersatzung*), which forms the basis for all other statutes. Thus, certain parts of the model statutes that have been declared mandatory must be included in each of the respective statutes.

44. A statute includes the following:

- concrete regulations on the internal organization of the respective social insurance institution; and
- extensions of benefits in favour of the insured persons if the legal provisions allow such room for manoeuvre; these are termed statutory additional benefits.

B. Health Regulations

45. Additionally, social insurance institutions are authorized and obliged to issue health insurance regulations (*Krankenordnungen*, §456 General Social Insurance Act). Just like statutes, these are regulations that are to be published on the Internet and approved by the federal minister responsible. Health insurance regulations contain provisions on services; in particular, they specify:

- the behaviour of the insured persons and beneficiaries in an insured event (e.g., during an illness);
- the control and monitoring of the insured persons; and
- the procedure for claiming benefits.

C. Guidelines of the Umbrella Organization of Social Insurance Institutions

46. By means of general directives (*Richtlinien des Dachverbandes der Sozialversicherungsträger*), the umbrella association must ensure that the enforcement of the social insurance institutions is carried out in a uniform, adequate and economically efficient manner. These guidelines are regulations and are published on the Internet; in some cases, they also require the approval of the competent federal minister. Examples of regulatory issues that can be addressed by such procedures are:

- service regulations and duty rosters;
- economic principles underlying the treatment and prescription of remedies; and
- exemption from the prescription fee.

D. Framework Agreements and Individual Contracts

47. The relationship between self-employed physicians and health insurance providers is regulated by a general framework agreement (*Gesamtvertrag*) and individual contracts (*Einzelvertrag*). Collective bargaining systems of this kind ensure that the interests of the service providers are protected and the best possible coverage of benefits in kind is ensured.

48. The framework agreement is concluded between the locally competent medical associations (*Ärztekammern*) and the Umbrella Organization of Social Insurance Institutions for the respective health insurance institutions; the individual contract is between the specific service provider and the relevant health insurance institution. The framework agreement has an absolute, two-sided binding effect. Its content – similar to a collective agreement in labour law – directly affects the individual contract, and the regulations are directly binding for the individual doctors (normative effect). The provisions on the conclusion of the contract itself have the effect of a contractual obligation.

IV. Social Security Procedures Law

49. On account of their legal nature, social security benefits by the insurance bodies are granted as public law allowances. This means that – at the first level – an executive body is competent as to the decision whether or not a denied benefit should be granted. Due to the lack of more specific rules, the *Allgemeine Verwaltungsverfahrensgesetz 1991* (*AVG*, BGBl. Nr. 51/1991) is applicable. The legal remedy against a negative decree from the social security body has to be brought before the courts (§367 General Social Insurance Act), which constitutes – at first sight – an exception to the principle of separation of the state powers; however, the courts do not decide on the basis of the administrative decree as such but decide the matter on their own account.

Chapter 4. Insured Persons

50. Since the mid-1990s, the main objective of the Austrian social security system has been the incorporation of all kinds of gainful employment into the compulsory social insurance system. The first motive was to protect more people by means of social insurance; another motive was securing the financing of the insurance system. Due to a broad incorporation of all types of gainful work, more people had to pay contributions.

51. The main groups of mandatorily insured persons are:

- employees;
- free employees and other forms of independent workers;
- the 'old' self-employed (with a trade licence) and the 'new' self-employed (without a trade licence);
- (self-employed) farmers;
- civil servants; and
- certain types of liberal professions (such as notaries, attorneys, architects and physicians).

52. Though the latter groups are all much smaller than the group of employees, they each have their own insurance system laid down in a proper statute and sometimes even a proper insurance institution.

53. For persons who are not included within one of the above-mentioned groups, there exists the possibility of voluntary insurance to avoid lack of protection; this form of insurance may apply, for example, to persons who do not work themselves and are too old to be co-insured as family members. Unlike *ex lege* insurance, people have to make a request to be voluntarily insured. Voluntary insurance comprises three forms: voluntary self-insurance (*Selbstversicherung*), voluntary continuation of insurance (*Weiterversicherung*) and increased insurance (*Höherversicherung*).

§1. Obligatorily Insured Persons

I. Employees

54. In general, employees are fully insured under the General Insurance Act, that is, within the branches of health insurance, accident insurance and pension insurance (for the exception, *see* General Introduction Chapter 4 §1 I B). According to §4 section 2 of this Act, an employee is someone working in a personal and economic relationship for money.

A. *Definition of Employee*

55. The status of an employee is connected closely to so-termed personal dependence: performing work in a state of personal dependence means that work is carried out in a position of subordination, in other words, under the command, authority and control of another and using the resources belonging to another, namely, the employer. Employees cannot freely decide when, where or which work they are to perform, as this depends on the employer's orders. Economic dependence in this sense means that an employee does not have at their disposal their own establishment, essential work equipment or even their own employees or subcontractors. Economically dependent people work with their employer's equipment under their control and authority. Furthermore, employees must be obliged to work in person; they are not allowed and not obliged to send a representative in the event of being prevented from working.

56. According to the legal definition, an employee has to carry out gainful employment to be included in social security. Social insurance under the *Bismarck* system and the principle of *ex lege* insurance refers to payment from which the level of contributions is derived.

B. *Full Insurance and Partial Insurance*

57. In general, employees earning more than the marginal monthly payment (in 2023: EUR 500.91) are fully insured, which includes health, pension and professional accident insurance in accordance with the General Social Insurance Act. Due to historical developments, currently, some employees or persons are only partially insured in accordance with this Act; the partial insurance may comprise one or two branches. Partial insurance in the field of health and accident insurance applies, for example, to some groups of employees of privatized enterprises and also to employed (= associate) or candidate lawyers; partial insurance in the field of health insurance applies to beneficiaries of unemployment allowances.

58. Furthermore, there is an exemption from full insurance for part-time workers who are marginally employed persons at the same time, that is, employees earning up to a maximum of EUR 500.91 per month (in 2023); such (free) employees are insured only in the field of accident insurance.

C. *Types of Employees*

59. In most cases, the insurance system does not distinguish between blue- and white-collar workers or other types of employees; they are all included within the term 'employee' in the sense of §4 section 2 General Insurance Act. A relevant exception to this equal treatment exists in the possibility of assigning someone to another job in the event that they are incapable of their former work (*see* Part V Chapter 2). As for the exempted marginally paid employees, *see* above.

D. Beginning and End of the Insurance Relationship

60. Due to the principle of *ex lege* insurance, the insurance relationship starts on 'the day of the beginning of the employment' (§10 section 1 General Insurance Act), regardless of adequate notification of the insurance body about the employment.

61. The insurance relationship ends at the same time as the employment relationship or, put more precisely, with the end of the claim for payment against the employer. First, there are constellations where the employment relationship is still operational but without a claim for payment, for example, in the case of strike or after the expiration of sick pay after a long illness. During such times, no contributions are paid. Second, the insurance is still in place, and contributions must be paid, although the employment relationship has ended, as long as the former employee has a claim for compensation for wrongful termination or leave that has not been taken.

62. Despite the ending of the employment or insurance relationship, the protection for the formerly insured person stays in place for a certain period (usually up to six weeks), however, in a reduced manner and only in the field of health protection.

E. Employer

63. Social insurance law also defines the other proponent of the social insurance relationship: the employer. An employer is the person in whose economic favour and on whose account the enterprise is operated. This applies also to a case where the employee gets parts of their payment from a third party (such as tips).

II. Free Employees

64. According to §4 section 4 of the General Insurance Act (which was not introduced until 1997), a free employee has the same status as an employee; consequently, free employees are fully insured under the terms of this Act, that is, in the branches of health insurance, accident insurance and pension insurance (for the exception of marginally paid free employees, *see* General Introduction Chapter 4 §1 I B).

65. A free employee is someone performing periodic services for others based on a contract under civil law but not in a position of (complete) personal dependence, that is to say, who is not subject to (comprehensive) command or control. Nevertheless, a free employee performs most of the time in person and has no working resources or materials of his or her own.

III. Specific Forms of Independent Workers

66. In accordance with explicit instructions in §4 section 1 nr. 3–14 of the General Insurance Act, several specific forms of non-employees have been protected by this Act in the same way as employees since its introduction. Full insurance, therefore, also applies, for example, to members of the board of a joint stock company (*Aktiengesellschaft* or *AG*) or limited liability company (*GmbH*), certain functionaries of the protestant churches or homeworkers.

IV. 'Old' Self-Employed Persons

67. Self-employed persons are defined in the Commercial Social Security Act (§2 section 1 nr. 1–3), referring to the fact that such people have a trade licence themselves or are shareholders or associates of companies organized in the form of a general partnership (*Offene Gesellschaft*), that is, members of the Commercial Chamber. Traditionally, this form of self-employment has been associated with merchants or salespersons, who are, therefore, nowadays also called 'old' self-employed. These types of self-employed persons are insured in the fields of health and pension insurance under the Commercial Social Security Act, whereas their accident insurance is laid down in the General Insurance Act (§8 section 1 nr. 3).

68. In general, the mandatory insurance relationship starts and ends in parallel with getting and giving up the trade licence for good; having no income, suffering losses, or even becoming insolvent does not end the insurance obligations as such.

V. 'New' Self-Employed Persons

69. The Commercial Social Security Act (§2 section 1 nr. 4) also incorporates the new self-employed persons, that is, people who perform services or generate countable work (such as writing one judicial article or painting two portraits) and get paid by their clients but do not perform work which would require a trade licence. Also, they are not members of the Commercial Chamber. Examples of such new self-employed are authors, freelance journalists, speakers, members of controlling boards, freelance midwives or carers and teachers.

70. Unlike the old self-employed, the new are only insured if their yearly income is in excess of the yearly marginal earnings threshold (in 2023: EUR 6,010.92 (12 x 500.91)); under this threshold and in the absence of any other income, there is no mandatory insurance.

VI. (Self-Employed) Farmers

71. Those who are self-employed in the field of agriculture (including the fields of land, forestry and livestock work) are insured in accordance with the Farmers'

Social Security Act. This type of self-employed insurance comprises all persons who conduct agricultural businesses at their own risk and on their own account (*Betriebsführer_in*); it does not only include land or forest owners but also tenants or leaseholders. Furthermore, family members such as spouses, children or parents who are (still) working on the farm (forest or land) are fully insured in all three branches of social insurance (i.e., health, pension and accident insurance); unlike other dependent employees, they are not insured in accordance with the General Insurance Act.

72. In general, the insurance relationship starts and ends in parallel with the beginning and end of the conducting of the agricultural business (farm, livestock establishment and so on).

VII. Civil Servants and Employees of (Former) Public Bodies

73. Civil servants (*Beamt_innen*) have a public law relationship to their employer, which is usually the state, one of the federal provinces or a (former) public body; such persons are appointed to their posts by decree. Besides civil servants, the state or other (former) public law bodies also have employees with whom they have made employment contracts (*Vertragsbedienstete*). Civil servants and contractual employees of public law bodies are insured in accordance with the Civil Servants Health and Accident Insurance Act in the field of health and accident insurance. Pensions are granted in accordance with the new pension system to all of them under the same regime; however, certain civil servants still fall under the social welfare system. For specific civil servants of cities or federal provinces, there also exist additional regulations and health institutions.

74. Certain public functionaries and representatives, such as members of parliament, (federal) government or city councils, mayors and so on are also insured in accordance with the Civil Servants Health and Accident Insurance Act.

75. Since 1 January 2020, the date when the reform of the social security organization became effective, a new group of employees has also been included: employees of the Austrian Railways Company and employees of other railway or traffic companies and mining companies are insured under the Civil Servants Health and Accident Insurance Act.

§2. Voluntarily Insured Persons

76. Voluntary insurance comprises three relevant forms: voluntary self-insurance (*Selbstversicherung*), voluntary continuation of insurance (*Weiterversicherung*) and increased insurance (*Höherversicherung*). In all these cases, people only become insured after a request to the insurance body, and they pay their contribution on their own account.

I. Persons with Self-Insurance

77. Each person with a residence in Austria is able to insure themself in the branch of health insurance with the Austrian Health Insurance Fund (§16 General Insurance Act); the same applies in the area of pension insurance (§16a General Insurance Act). By this means, people are able to remargin contributions to the pension system in case they lack contribution periods. Examples of self-insured people are students or (free) employees with income below the marginal earnings threshold.

II. Persons with Continued Self-Insurance

78. After the end of *ex lege* insurance, employees can continue to pay contributions on their own to avoid lack of qualifying periods for their pension (§17 General Insurance Act); the employee has to make a request for continuation within six months.

III. Persons with Increased Self-Insurance

79. Employees are able to increase their pensions by additional voluntary contributions to pension insurance (§248 General Insurance Act).

IV. Formally Insured Persons

80. For people having doubts as to whether or not they fulfil the criteria for an insurance relationship, there exists the possibility of formal insurance. The objective of formal insurance is the protection of good faith of the insured person. Furthermore, if somebody is not insured under false pretences and contributions are paid and accepted by the insurance agency, this leads to a formal insurance – with the consequence of being insured till the designation of insurance by decree. Examples of formally insured persons are spouses who work in the business of their wives or husbands due to matrimonial duties and without having made an employment contract.

Part I. The Institutions

81. A variety of authorities and legal bodies are competent for the enforcement of 'social law'; this is because the term 'social law' as such cannot be found in the constitutional provisions of the Federal Constitutional Law on federal and state competences. There are several competences in specific areas of social law, such as 'social insurance', 'hospitals', 'the poor' or 'nursing allowance.' As a result, both federal and state responsibilities exist not only in the area of legislation but also in the area of the executive bodies. In addition, social security law is partly implemented by special administrative bodies that are not state authorities but rather the following self-governing institutions.

Chapter 1. Highest Administrative Bodies and Representatives

82. The highest administrative representative at federal level is, according to its current designation, the Federal Minister for Social Affairs, Health, Care and Consumer Protection. The Minister is responsible for the administration of social security matters, including health insurance and accident insurance, which includes the supervision of the social insurance institutions. Other responsibilities include the coordination of long-term care and healthcare matters, including the monitoring and control of infectious diseases – which is particularly relevant from today's perspective – as well as performance-based financing of health services, health reporting, quality of healthcare, health informatics and health telematics.

83. In other areas of social law, however, the Federal Minister of Labour, Family and Youth is the highest body; his or her authority – including the corresponding powers of instruction and supervision – covers matters relating to the labour market in particular and, therefore, also unemployment insurance.

Chapter 2. Social Insurance Institutions

84. The most important administrative bodies in the area of social law are the social insurance institutions, which, as self-governing bodies under the supervision of the federal government, administer the affairs of the insured persons and their relatives. In contrast to an administrative body that is purely governmental, self-administration means that the parties concerned (in this case, the insured persons) are directly involved in the administration of social insurance. They are legal entities under public law, through which the respective profession organizes the insurance itself, and the federal government has only the right to supervise the administration (*see* §448 section 1 *ASVG*). In practice, self-administration is carried out by indirect representation through the delegation of representatives of the respective occupational groups by the interest groups or social partners (especially Labour Unions and Trade Unions). In their area of responsibility, these self-governing bodies operate free of directives and act as sovereign bodies; they can also issue decisions and regulations.

85. The main task of social insurance institutions is the implementation of social law within their area of application. Regarding the organization of the social insurance institutions, a basic distinction is made between the insurance branch and the occupational groups covered. The social insurance institutions are mainly divided into health insurance institutions, accident insurance institutions and pension insurance institutions. Health insurance institutions are mainly responsible for the organization and provision of medical treatment. This is achieved through cooperation with and the conclusion of contracts with the associations representing the interests of the various medical professions (such as medical associations, midwifery committees or dental associations), which ensure that a sufficient number of general practitioners, specialists, physiotherapists, midwives and so forth are available to the insured persons in a certain region. In addition to this, health insurance institutions may also establish and operate their own hospitals or similar institutions, including the establishment of outpatient clinics. The accident insurance institutions are responsible for accident prevention and first aid provision, including the relevant training; furthermore, the accident insurance institutions run special hospitals and rehabilitation facilities for accidents at work and occupational diseases. In addition to the organization of pension insurance, the pension insurance institutions are also responsible for the establishment of suitable rehabilitation institutions. Moreover, they must pay the contributions to the health insurance of pensioners.

86. Due to the Organizational Reform of 2018, BGBl. I Nr. 100/2018, only five of the original twenty-one social insurance institutions remain. These are:

(1) The Austrian Health Insurance Fund (*Österreichische Gesundheitskasse, ÖGK*), the health insurance institution for employees. This health insurance institution, which now operates nationwide, was created from the merger of the former nine regional health insurance funds (*Gebietskrankenkassen,*

GKK), each of which was responsible for only one federal state. In addition, five company health insurance funds (*Betriebskrankenkasse, BKK*) were incorporated into it.

(2) The Pension Insurance Institution (*Pensionsversicherungsanstalt, PVA*) which is responsible for the pension insurance of employees.

(3) The General Accident Insurance Institution (*Allgemeine Unfallversicherungsanstalt, AUVA*), which is responsible for the accident insurance of employees.

(4) The Social Security Institution for the self-employed (*Sozialversicherungsanstalt der Selbständigen, SVS*), for self-employed farmers and foresters (covered by health insurance and pension insurance in accordance with the Farmers' Social Security Act, covered by accident insurance in accordance with the General Social Insurance Act) as well as the self-employed (covered by health insurance and pension insurance in accordance with the Commercial Social Security Act, covered by accident insurance in accordance with the General Social Insurance Act). It was formed by merging the Social Insurance Institution of the Industrial Economy (*Sozialversicherungsanstalt der gewerblichen Wirtschaft, SVA*) and the Social Security Institution for Farmers (*Sozialversicherungsanstalt der Bauern, SVB*).

(5) The Social Insurance Institution for Civil Servants and Employees in the area of Railways and Mining (*Versicherungsanstalt öffentlich Bediensteter, Eisenbahnen und Bergbau, BVAEB*). It was created by merging the Insurance Institution for Civil Servants (*Versicherungsanstalt der öffentlich Bediensteten, BVA*) and the Insurance Institution for Railways and Mining (*Versicherungsanstalt für Eisenbahnen und Bergbau, VAEB*).

All social insurance institutions combined form the umbrella organization of the Austrian social insurance institutions, the *Dachverband der Sozialversicherungsträger* (§§30 et seq. General Social Insurance Act; formerly: *Hauptverband der Sozialversicherungsträger*). This organization is also a corporation under public law and represents the interests of its members, in other words, the social insurance institutions, externally.

Chapter 3. Other Authorities

87. In the area of unemployment insurance, the Public Employment Service is responsible for administration. It is a public legal body and a federal authoritative body that is under the directive of the federal minister, but – unlike the other social insurance agencies – it is not a self-governing body.

Part II. Contribution and Financing

88. In social security law, according to the idea of *Bismarck*, social insurance is basically financed by the contributions of the insured persons and their employers. In addition to this, however, in some branches of insurance, there are now also co-payments by the state because the contributions themselves are not sufficient. This applies particularly in the field of pension insurance.

89. The obligation to pay the contributions is determined by the law applicable to the respective group of insured persons (principle of *ex lege* insurance). The amount thereof, that is, the percentage level, meaning the contribution rates, is also set by law. The basis for the calculation of contributions (*Beitragsgrundlage*) is always the income of the person insured under the social insurance scheme, from the amount of which certain percentages are calculated and then paid as contributions to the social security body. There is, however, a maximum limit for the contribution base, up to which income is used in the calculation (maximum contribution base, *Höchstbeitragsgrundlage*). Income above this level does not count, and no contributions need to be paid from that.

Chapter 1. Contribution Law of Employees and Free Employees

90. The basis for the contributions of (free) employees is their remuneration, meaning the remuneration that the employer has to pay the (free) employee for the provision of the contractually owed services. Here, the '*debit* principle' is applied (*Anspruchslohnprinzip*): The basis for contributions is the remuneration to which the (free) employee concerned has a legal or contractual entitlement, as well as any payment in cash or in kind actually provided by the employer without the (free) employee being entitled to them. If the employer paid less than the employee was entitled to, this would, therefore, be irrelevant, and the amount of the actually owed payment would be the basis for the contribution.

§1. Basis of Contribution: (Free) Employee's Payment

91. The types of payment that are part of the remuneration are defined in §§49 and 50 General Social Insurance Act. The definition of the relevant remuneration includes both cash and non-cash benefits, namely monthly basic pay, commissions, overtime bonuses or special payments, as well as company cell phones, company cars or a company apartment. What are not to be taken as a basis are mainly the compensation of expenses (reimbursement of expenses), but also certain forms of remuneration or combinations of remuneration and compensation of expenses, such as reimbursement of travel expenses, certain allowances and grants, subsidized meals or drinks at the company and severance payments.

92. The remuneration, in accordance with §49 General Social Insurance Act, forms the contribution basis from which the contribution rates are calculated by the employer and then paid to the social insurance agency. The contribution base has an upper limit; for all insurance branches, the maximum contribution base is EUR 5,850.00 per month or EUR 195.00 per day (status: 2023; *see* §45 General Social Insurance Act).

§2. Size of Contribution

93. As regards the employees and free employees, the contributions to health insurance, pension insurance and unemployment insurance are divided between the employer and the employee; the contribution to accident insurance must be paid only by the employer. Furthermore, the contribution rates, that is, the percentages of the contribution basis, vary depending on the insurance branch (§§51 et seq. General Social Insurance Act).

Health insurance 7.65%
(blue-collar worker: employer = 3.87%: 3.78%;
white-collar worker: employer = 3.87%: 3.78%;
free employee: employer = 3.87%: 3.78%)
(retirees: 5.10%)

Accident insurance 1.10%
(to be paid by the employer)

Pension insurance 22.80%
(all kinds of employee: employer = 10.25%: 12.55%)

Unemployment insurance 6.00%
(all kinds of employee: employer = 3.00%: 3.00%
apprentice: employer = 1.20%: 1.20%)

94. Other imposts to be delivered together with the social insurance contributions are the following:

– surcharge for insolvency fee protection (*IESG-Zuschlag*) 0.10% (to be paid by the employer);
– Chamber of Labour impost (*Arbeiterkammerumlage*) 0.50% (to be paid by the employee);
– housing promotion contribution (only for employees, not for free employees) 1.00% (employee: employer = 0.50: 0.50); and
– employer's levy; employers who employ several marginally employed (free) workers whose total wages exceed 1.5 times the marginal earnings threshold (i.e., in 2023, EUR 751.37) must pay a flat-rate employer's impost for these employees (§1 Employer Levy Act). The amount of the employer's impost is 16.4% of the total payroll of all who are marginally employed by this employer. This impost is to be paid in addition to the accident insurance contribution of 0.10% for the respective (free) employee.

Chapter 2. Contribution Law for Self-Employed Persons

§1. Self-Employed Persons under the Commercial Social Security Act

95. Self-employed persons who are insured under the Commercial Social Security Act (and the Freelance Social Security Act as well) pay contributions to the social security system, which are determined by the level of their income. This is called the '*inflow* principle' (*Zuflussprinzip*). The income, according to the income tax assessment, is taken into account, meaning the profits (= income minus expenses) which the self-employed person has made in a calendar year. Only the new self-employed have an additional income limit, which must be exceeded in order to be covered by social insurance in accordance with the Commercial Social Security Act.

96. As the residual profit in a running calendar year would be uncertain, the current contributions of the self-employed are calculated on the basis of the income tax assessment from the third preceding calendar year; it is, therefore, only a provisional monthly contribution basis. If the self-employed person had no (independent) income three years ago, the contributions are calculated from the minimum contribution base (*Mindestbeitragsgrundlage*). The final contribution base replaces the provisional contribution base when the income tax assessment for the respective year is available. Subsequently, the contributions are to be calculated according to the actual profits; therefore, additional payment of contributions may be required if the amount of contributions paid for the year in question is too low.

97. The concept of the minimum contribution base aims to ensure that self-employed persons have to pay social security contributions in any case, regardless of whether they have profits or losses. The minimum contribution base is based on the marginal earnings threshold so that self-employed persons must pay contributions towards health insurance, accident insurance and pension insurance at least for a fictitious profit of EUR 500.91 (status: 2023). A reduced minimum contribution basis exists for young entrepreneurs in their founding and initial phase; there are also exceptions for older self-employed persons over 57 or persons who have already reached the standard retirement age and are still self-employed. In addition, the maximum contribution basis up to which the contributions are calculated must be observed; beyond this, the income is non-contributory (status 2023: EUR 6,825.00).

98. The contribution rates for self-employed persons are (§§27, 29 Commercial Social Security Act; §8 Liberal Professions Social Security Act):

Health insurance self-employed persons: 7.65% (insured persons: 6.80%, rest: tax revenue)
retirees: 5.10%
Accident insurance EUR 10.97 per month (status: 2023)
Pension insurance 22.80% (insured persons *GSVG* 18.50%, rest: tax money; insured persons *FSVG* 20%, rest: tax money).

§2. Self-Employed Persons under the Farmers' Social Security Act

99. Farmers and foresters, in accordance with the Farmers' Social Security Act, have to pay contributions to the social insurance, which – as with the self-employed or employees – are based on income. The basis for contributions is generally based on the size of the farmer's business, which is determined in the form of a notice as a (tax-calculated) unit value (§23 section 2). The respective unit value of the relevant farm is subsequently valorized each year for the purpose of paying the contribution. There exists a minimum unit value (*Mindesteinheitswert*), which is EUR 1,500.00 for health insurance and pension insurance, and for accident insurance, EUR 150.00 per year.

100. There is a second way that farmers and foresters can pay contributions. Insured persons can also base their contributions on the actual income of the year concerned (termed contribution base option (*Beitragsgrundlagenoption*), §23 section 1a Farmers' Social Security Act); in this case, the contributions are calculated on the basis of the income statement.

101. The contribution rates are (§§24, 26 Farmers' Social Security Act):

Health insurance self-employed persons: 7.65% (insured persons: 6.80%, rest: tax revenue)
retirees: 5.60%
Accident insurance 1.90%
Pension insurance 22.80% (insured persons 17%, rest: tax revenue; insured persons *FSVG* 20%, rest: tax revenue).

Part III. Healthcare

Chapter 1. General Introduction and Field of Application

§1. General Structure, Principals and Territorial Field of Application

102. As regards health insurance, the place of employment, not one's citizenship, is decisive. People commuting from another country to work in Austria are covered by Austrian social insurance.

I. Occupational Affiliation and Competent Insurance Institutions

103. The Austrian social security system is organized by profession. In other words, affiliation to a certain institution depends on one's occupational activity. Since 1 January 2020, the health insurance institutions administering the health insurance system are:

- the Austrian Health Insurance Fund (*ÖGK*) for employed persons, all pensioners previously insured with the nine regional health insurance funds (*Gebietskrankenkassen*), and all persons previously insured with a company health insurance fund (*Betriebskrankenkasse*);
- the Social Security Institution for the self-employed (*SVS*), for the self-employed and liberal professions previously insured with the Social Insurance Institution of the Industrial Economy (*SVA*), as well as for self-employed farmers and foresters previously insured with the Social Security Institution for farmers (*SVB*); and
- the Social Security Institution for civil servants, employees in the area of railways and mining (*BVAEB*) for those previously insured with the former Insurance Institution for railways and mining (*VAEB*) and for civil servants and contract staff previously insured with the Insurance Institution for Civil Servants (*BVA*) employed after 31 December 2000, as long as they do not belong to a Healthcare Institution (*Krankenfürsorgeanstalt, KFA*) established at state level.

II. Principle of Finality

104. The principle of finality means that the insured event is basically independent of the cause that led to the illness or (temporary) incapacity to work.

The incapacity to work does not have to be related to gainful employment – in contrast to the accident insurance scheme; however, there are exceptions to the principle of finality insofar as, for example, people are not entitled to certain health insurance benefits for injuries caused by alcohol consumption or leisure activities in the mountains.

§2. Personal Scope of Application

I. Insured Persons

105. Health insurance is closely linked to employment. In health insurance, primarily all gainfully employed persons, especially employees and all self-employed persons of all types, are covered. Contributions to health insurance are based on the level of income; however, to be covered by health insurance, the income must be above what is called the marginal earnings threshold (2023: EUR 500.91 per month).

106. In principle, the insured persons themselves pay contributions to their respective insurance institution; however, in the case of employees, both the employee and the employer make contributions to social insurance and, therefore, also to health insurance. Employees' contributions are deducted from their gross income (remuneration) and transferred to the social insurance fund together with the contributions paid by the employer.

II. Co-insured Persons

107. In addition to the employed persons in the field of health insurance, their relatives may also be entitled to benefits. This is known as co-insurance. Such relatives may not, however, be covered by statutory health insurance themselves, that is, as long as the relatives are not employed themselves or are incapable of work. In addition, they must have their habitual residence in Austria. According to §123 General Social Insurance Act (§83 Commercial Social Security Act, §78 Farmers' Social Security Act, §56 Civil Servants Health and Accident Insurance Law), the following count as co-insured persons:

- Current spouses.
- Children, adopted children, stepchildren or grandchildren under 18 (in some cases, however, only if they live in the same household as the insured person).
- Children, adopted children or stepchildren over 18 (in principle until the end of their education, up to 27 years of age).
- Life partners (if they run the household and have been living in the same household for at least ten months).

108. In general, co-insurance is contribution-free. The family members do not pay any contributions of their own, and the contributions of the employed persons are not higher if several members of the family are co-insured; however, the insured person must pay what is termed an additional contribution for spouses not having raised or currently raising any children of their own which amounts to 3.4% of the contribution base (§51d General Social Insurance Act, §27c Commercial Social Security Act, §24b Farmers' Social Security Act, §20b Civil Servants Health and Accident Insurance Law).

109. A premium-free co-insurance is also available for caring relatives (§51d section 3 No. 3 General Social Insurance Act, §27c section 3 No. 3 Commercial Social Security Act, §24b section 3 No. 3 Farmers' Social Security Act, §20b section 3 No. 3 Civil Servants Health and Accident Insurance Law). The term 'relatives' is broader and also includes persons who are not normally eligible for non-contributory co-insurance, such as siblings or in-laws. To qualify, the person in need of care must be entitled to a care allowance of at least Level Three, and the home-based care must take up the majority of the relative's resources.

III. Other Economically Inactive but Insured Persons

110. The protection of compulsory health insurance also applies to certain persons who are not employed, especially unemployed or retired persons.

Chapter 2. Events Insured and Benefits

§1. General Information

111. The health insurance covers the following insured events: illness, incapacity (temporary or reduced) to work due to illness, pregnancy and maternity. Reintegration after a long period of sickness has now been added to these key areas. In addition, it is also the task of health insurance to take measures to prevent and avoid illness and to strengthen health.

112. The benefits to which the insured persons are entitled under these circumstances, such as medical treatment, are not always provided directly by the health insurance institution itself, however. The health insurance institutions organize and provide their services to the insured persons by employing doctors or other medical staff (physiotherapists, psychologists, midwives, etc.), pharmacies or hospitals (*Sachleistungsprinzip*, the principle of benefits in kind). The legal relationship between these persons or institutions and the health insurance institutions is regulated by contracts (framework agreements and individual contracts, *see* General Introduction Chapter 3 §2 III). Accordingly, the persons involved are referred to as contract physicians or contract group practices (*see also* Part III Chapter 2 §2). If a sick, insured person visits a 'contract physician', the patient does not have to pay the costs himself or herself but only has to show the electronic health insurance card, commonly known as an e-card. The costs of the medical examination or treatment are settled between the social insurance agency and the attending physician. Benefits that are provided by social security are called benefits in kind (*Sachleistungen*), while cash benefits (*Geldleistungen*) are paid directly to insured persons by the social insurance institution.

113. In terms of benefits, a further distinction must be made between compulsory (*Pflichtleistungen*) and voluntary (*freiwillige Leistungen*) health insurance benefits:

- Compulsory benefits may be provided by law or by the statutes established by the respective health insurance institution; for statutes, *see* General Introduction Chapter 3 §2 III. Individuals are entitled to the compulsory benefit, which can be enforced through legal action.
- Voluntary benefits may only be provided by the social security institution if the institution has been legally authorized to do so. Individuals are not automatically entitled to voluntary benefits (such as a subsidy for a stay at a health resort); however, their discretionary powers may be reviewed by the courts.

§2. ILLNESS

I. Definitions

A. *Legal Term*

114. Social security law provides a definition of the concept of illness (*Krankheit*) – in contrast to labour law. According to §120 General Social Insurance Act, it is a condition of the body or mind *contrary to the rules* which require medical treatment (literal translation of *regelwidriger Körper- oder Geisteszustand*, also laid down in §80 Commercial Social Security Act, §76 Farmers' Social Security Act, §53 Civil Servants Health and Accident Insurance Law). *Contrary to rules* means – carefully summarized – that the condition of the sick person deviates from a medical ideal. A treatment is regarded as necessary if it can restore or at least improve the health or ability to work of the ill person. Examples are rhinitis, cancer, broken limbs, various mental illnesses such as schizophrenia and personality disorders, but also speech disorders, protruding ears or erectile dysfunction.

B. *Illness in Contrast to Impairment*

115. If a physical or mental impairment cannot be cured or at least controlled by medical treatment, it is not considered to be an illness but rather an impairment (*Gebrechen*, §154 General Social Insurance Act, §93 Commercial Social Security Act, §96 Farmers' Social Security Act, §65 Civil Servants Health and Accident Insurance Law). This applies in particular to physical disorders or failure of bodily functions. Examples are hearing loss, tooth loss, bladder weakness or myopia.

II. Benefits

116. Benefits in the event of sickness comprise benefits in kind and cash benefits. In principle, both insured persons who are gainfully employed and their co-insured relatives are legally entitled to benefits in kind, irrespective of the amount of their health insurance contribution; all insured persons are equally entitled (e.g., to medical treatment in a hospital). In contrast, only employed insured persons receive cash benefits, partly depending also, indirectly, on their contributions to the health insurance scheme, which are linked to the amount of their income.

117. Sickness benefits in kind, which appertain to insured and co-insured persons likewise, include:

– medical treatment (*Krankenbehandlung*);
– institutional care (*Anstaltspflege*); and
– medical home nursing (Medizinische Hauskrankenpflege).

A. Medical Treatment

118. The aim of healthcare is to restore, strengthen or improve the insured person's health, capacity to work and ability to care for themself (§133 section 2 General Social Insurance Act, §90 section 2 Commercial Social Security Act, §83 section 2 Farmers' Social Security Act, §62 section 2 Civil Servants Health and Accident Insurance Law). The medical treatment must be sufficient and appropriate, however, and it must not exceed what is necessary to ensure that resources are used economically and efficiently. According to case law, there is no entitlement to the world's best medicine, but the treatment has to offer at least a sufficient chance of cure. If the results seem to be similar, the method that costs the least should be chosen.

119. Medical treatment includes:

- medical assistance (*Ärztliche Hilfe*) and services equivalent to medical care, for example, psychotherapy, clinical psychology or physiotherapy; and
- remedies (*Heilmittel*) and medical aids (*Heilbehelfe*).

120. Medical assistance is provided:

- by individual doctors or by a group of doctors in their own practice who have a contract with the health insurance institution (*Vertragsärzte*, contract doctors; *Vertragsgruppenpraxen*, contract group practices); or by
- individual doctors or groups of doctors in their practice not affiliated with a health insurance institution (*Wahlärzte*, doctors of choice; *Wahlarztgruppenpraxen*, group practices of doctors of choice); or in
- the social insurance institution's own facilities (*Ambulatorien*, outpatient clinics).

121. The insured persons have the right to choose a doctor freely (*Recht auf freie Arztwahl*); they can decide which doctor should provide the medical treatment. In the case of contract physicians, patients show what is called an e-card, a special identity card which is proof of insurance. The social insurance institution will then pay for the doctor's visit or outpatient clinic visit directly. In the case of physicians without a contract with a health insurance company, the respective patients have to bear the costs of the treatment themselves and will be reimbursed afterwards in line with the tariff of the social insurance company.

122. Remedies for the treatment of illnesses primarily involve the prescription of medication. If medicines are prescribed by a doctor, their cost is borne by the social insurance institution. Patients only have to pay a socially acceptable contribution, the 'prescription fee' (*Rezeptgebühr*); in 2023, it amounts to EUR 6.85 per drug.

123. Medical aids are intended to compensate for or replace lacking or impaired bodily functions of the insured person. Examples of these are: hearing aids, glasses, contact lenses or orthopaedic shoes. Medical aids are granted in a simple and practical form; the insured must usually pay a small deductible.

B. Institutional Care

124. In the case of institutional care (§§144–150 General Social Insurance Act, §§96–98 Commercial Social Security Act, §§89–93 Farmers' Social Security Act, §§66–68 Civil Servants Health and Accident Insurance Law), the patient is treated as an inpatient, that is to say, the ill person stays overnight and eats in the hospital. Hospitals are medical facilities that serve to determine, monitor or restore the state of health. Nursing care is provided, in particular, through extensive medical examinations and by carrying out surgical interventions, as well as through the delivery or provision of remedies.

125. In principle, a referral (*Überweisung*) by a contract physician is required; however, in emergencies, it is also provided without such a referral (for instance, §145 General Social Insurance Act, §90 Farmers' Social Security Act). Furthermore, it is necessary that the patient requires medical treatment. If – for instance, due to the patient's signs of old age – only care and assistance with everyday tasks is necessary (termed *Asylierung*), there is no entitlement for social insurance to cover the costs of the stay in the hospital.

126. A differentiation must be made between public hospitals (*öffentliche Krankenanstalten*), nursing homes (*Pflegeanstalten*) and sanatoriums (*Sanatorien*). Nursing homes are facilities for chronically ill or old people in need of constant medical and specialist care. Sanatoriums are hospitals which, due to their specialist equipment, meet higher standards with regard to food and accommodation and are regularly operated by private institutions. In some cases, however, public hospitals also offer higher standards of board and accommodation – such as double rooms instead of six-bed rooms – to people who have private supplementary insurance (*private Zusatzversicherung*).

C. Medical Home Nursing

127. Medical home nursing (*Medizinische Hauskrankenpflege*, §151 General Social Insurance Act, §99 Commercial Social Security Act, §94 Farmers' Social Security Act, §71 Civil Servants Health and Accident Insurance Law) is a type of care that is intended to substitute for a hospital stay. In addition to the necessary medical treatment and medication, it provides care and nursing in a familiar home environment instead of in a hospital. The care at home is carried out by qualified nursing staff.

128. Medical home nursing care is provided on medical orders and only includes medical services and qualified nursing services such as Decubitus care (wound care), injections, tube feeding or stoma, fistula and catheter care.

129. Medical home nursing does not include, for example, services such as skin, hair and dental care or bedpan handling, as well as assistance with daily and domestic needs (such as making beds, changing beds or cooking meals). These services are not reimbursed by social insurance. If necessary, a nursing allowance (*Pflegegeld*) may be provided for these expenses (*see* Part X Chapter 2).

130. The maximum duration of home medical care for the same illness is limited to four weeks; for this period, no authorization is required. It can be extended after approval by the specific medical controlling staff of the competent health insurance body (*Chef- und Kontrollärztlicher Dienst*).

D. Dental Treatment, Dentures, Orthodontic Treatment

131. Health disorders affecting one's teeth also fall under the definition of illness; consequently, dental treatment would constitute a form of medical treatment; however, benefits granted for medical conditions involving teeth are regulated separately from other medical treatment (§§153, 153a General Social Insurance Act, §§94, 94a Commercial Social Security Act, §§95, 95a Farmers' Social Security Act, §§69, 69a Civil Servants Health and Accident Insurance Law). Furthermore, the medical services and benefits are generally provided by dentists who graduate from universities in dentistry, which is a kind of medical study. Dentists offer medical assistance as contract or elective doctors or as doctors of a group practice or outpatient clinic.

132. Dental treatment can consist of surgical dental treatment or conservative dental treatment, as well as indispensable dental prostheses or jaw adjustments. It should be noted, however, that jaw adjustments are only granted as a benefit in kind by the social security system if the patient is under 18 years of age or – regardless of age – if the adjustment is necessary to prevent serious damage to health or to remove disfigurements that are likely to interfere with the patient's occupation. More detailed regulations on the conditions for granting surgical and conservative dental treatment can be found in the statutes of the respective competent social insurance institutions.

E. Transport to a Medical Facility

133. Transportation to a medical facility for the purpose of receiving medical assistance or institutional care is provided as a health insurance benefit in the form of vouchers for taxis or by covering the costs of an ambulance or helicopter. As a rule, there has to be an emergency case, which means that there has to be a sufficient suspicion of illness to justify the ambulance or helicopter being called and the transport taking place. More detailed regulations are laid down in the statutes of the respective social insurance institutions; it should be noted that rescue costs, for example, which are caused by sports or excursions in the mountains, are not covered by social insurance.

F. Remedies in the Case of Impairment

134. This includes objects or devices that replace parts of the body or body functions that have failed and can no longer be treated. Such remedies are only provided by law as voluntary benefits. Examples are hearing aids, cosmetic cover creams or reading glasses.

G. Medical Rehabilitation

135. Following urgent medical treatment, medical rehabilitation is provided to ensure and stabilize the health status of the patient. Above all, medical rehabilitation serves to eliminate or improve functional limitations resulting from one's illness, to reduce risk factors (secondary prevention), and to maintain one's ability to work. Furthermore, it is intended to avoid the need for long-term care or to maintain or improve the status of the need for long-term care. The most important purpose of rehabilitation is to enable the patient to participate in social and economic life independently and permanently. Illnesses that are treated during a stay at a rehabilitation resort, for example, include diseases of the musculoskeletal system, metabolic diseases or respiratory diseases. Medical rehabilitation is provided in health resorts or rehabilitation centres; it can be carried out either as an inpatient or an outpatient treatment. Medical rehabilitation measures must be necessary for medical reasons; they must be prescribed by a doctor and approved by the social insurance institution. In principle, patients have to contribute to the costs of the treatment, the amount depending on their personal circumstances.

§3. Incapacity to Work Due to Illness

I. Definition

136. For the term 'incapacity to work', there is – in contrast to illness – no legal definition laid down in the General Social Insurance Act. When interpreted systematically, this insured event only affects employed persons, as there must be a close connection with work. An ill employee or free employee is incapable of working if, as a result of their impairment of health, they are unable to provide the contractually owed benefits, or it is only possible to pursue the previously performed activity while risking a worsening of their condition.

137. Regarding incapacity to work due to illness, the contrast to permanent or long-term incapacity to work has to be pointed out: if an employee is permanently disabled or incapacitated for work, he or she may be entitled to an invalidity pension (blue-collar workers) or occupational disability pension (white-collar workers; *see* Part V Chapter 2 §4).

138. A so-termed partial capacity to work has no valid existence; either an employee is able to work or not. If an employee is employed by two or more employers, however, his capacity to work must be examined separately in connection with each activity contractually agreed upon.

139. The beginning and end of one's incapacity to work must always be determined by a physician having a contract with the social insurance institution responsible for the employee or free employee.

II. Benefits

140. In the case of incapacity to work, the employed person or free employee is entitled to all sickness benefits in kind which are due in the insured event of illness and which serve to cure the illness (e.g., medical treatment by a physician or in a hospital; *see* Part III Chapter 2 §2 II). In addition, he or she is also entitled to a cash benefit, the sickness allowance (*Krankengeld*), which is only granted to working people and not the co-insured. The aim of this benefit is to compensate for the financial losses caused by the illness.

141. Its amount is determined by:

- the calculation base; and
- the duration of the incapacity for work.

142. The calculation base for the sickness allowance is the gross remuneration of the last calendar month subject to social insurance contributions before the employee's full remuneration entitlement ends. Additional payments are taken into account in the form of a proportional supplement.

A. Sickness Allowance

1. Employees

143. The sickness allowance for employees is regulated in §§138 et seq. General Social Security Act. Employed persons are entitled to a sickness allowance from the fourth to the forty-second day of incapacity to work at the rate of 50% of their remuneration (more precisely, of the calculation base, *see* above); from the forty-third day, it amounts to 60% (§141, §125 General Social Insurance Act). During the first three days, there is no entitlement to this kind of cash benefit; however, certain labour regulations play an important role in this context, highlighting the interaction of labour law and social security law.

144. For the time an employee is sick, the employer must continue to pay at least six weeks of full remuneration and four weeks of 50%. This results from labour law regulations (§8 *Angestelltengesetz*; §2 *Entgeltfortzahlungsgesetz*). While the employer continues to pay 50% of the employee's remuneration, the employee also receives 50% of sickness benefit from the social insurance institution (*ÖGK*, Austrian Health Insurance Fund). When the continued payment of remuneration by the employer ends, employees receive the full sickness allowance from the Austrian Social Insurance Fund.

145. In other words, the entitlement to sickness allowance is suspended for as long as the sick employee is entitled to continued payment of more than 50% of the full remuneration in cash or in kind by the employer; if 50% of the full remuneration in cash or in kind is paid, half of the sickness allowance is suspended. If the employee receives less than 50% of the remuneration, he or she is entitled to the full amount of sickness allowance.

146. Sickness allowance is generally granted for up to twenty-six weeks. This entitlement period increases to fifty-two weeks if the insured persons were insured for six months within the last twelve months before the insured event occurred; furthermore, it may increase up to seventy-eight weeks if laid down by the statute of the competent sickness insurance institution.

147. Sickness allowance is, however, due until the end of the calendar month in which a decision is delivered concerning the award of a pension, an agreement concerning the granting of an advanced pension payment under the pension insurance scheme, or the granting of a provisional benefit.

2. Free Employees

148. Just like employees, free employees (also known as quasi-employees) receive a sickness allowance from the fourth day of work incapacity; however, they are not entitled to continued remuneration by their employer for the first three days since the above-described labour regulations do not apply.

3. Unemployed Persons

149. Recipients of benefits from unemployment insurance (e.g., unemployment benefit or emergency unemployment assistance) are entitled to sickness allowance from the fourth day of sickness or incapacity to work at the level of the last benefit received. An increase from the forty-third day of sickness is not available for this group of persons. For the first three days of sickness or incapacity to work, they continue to receive their unemployment insurance benefits (e.g., unemployment benefit, emergency unemployment assistance).

4. Marginally Employed Persons

150. Marginally employed persons (monthly marginal threshold in 2023: EUR 500.91) are generally only insured in the field of accident insurance (*see* General

Introduction Chapter 4 §1 I B). That is why only the marginally employed persons who have concluded a self-insurance policy in accordance with §19a General Social Insurance Act receive a fixed amount from the fourth day of sick leave (2023: EUR 6.00 per day). An increase in sickness benefits from the forty-third day onwards is not available for this group of persons.

5. Self-Employed Persons

151. Only if a self-employed person has subscribed to supplementary insurance for sickness benefits (§9 of the Commercial Social Security Act) will he or she receive a sickness allowance in accordance with §§105 et seq. Commercial Social Security Act. The entitlement to such an allowance accrues six months from the beginning of the supplementary insurance. Then, the self-employed person is entitled to sickness allowance from the fourth day of sickness or incapacity to work.

152. Apart from this voluntary insurance option, the Commercial Social Security Act provides for the following cash benefit under certain conditions in the event of incapacity to work: the entitlement is similar to the sickness allowance for employed persons but was introduced much later on 1 January 2013. It is called support benefit in the event of prolonged illness (*Unterstützungsleistung bei lang andauernder Krankheit*, §104a of the Commercial Social Security Act).

153. Those eligible are self-employed persons according to §104a section 2 of the Commercial Social Security Act:

- who are incapable of work for more than forty-two days at a time due to illness;
- whose professional performance is necessary for the maintenance of the business; and
- who usually employ fewer than twenty-five employees (including part-time employees).

154. The benefit is due for a period of a maximum of twenty weeks for the same illness retroactively from the fourth day onwards. The cash benefit amounts to EUR 33.98 per day (valid for 2023), irrespective of his or her income; this amount is adjusted annually.

6. Grounds for Exclusion from Sickness Allowance

155. No sickness benefit is due to the incapacity to work:

- is directly related to intoxication or substance abuse; or
- is caused by culpable participation in a brawl, and the ill person has been convicted legally, binding in this respect (§142 section 1 of the General Social Security Act).

B. Rehabilitation Allowance

156. If an employee is temporarily disabled or incapable of working for at least six months due to health impairment and is entitled to medical rehabilitation, the employee receives a rehabilitation allowance from the Austrian Health Insurance Fund instead of a temporary disability or occupational disability pension. Systematically, the rehabilitation benefit is a cash benefit paid by the health insurance fund (§143a General Social Insurance Act). Due to the close link with an occupational disability, however, the pension insurance fund is de facto and financially responsible (for instance, in granting the allowance, *see* §143a section 1 last sentence General Social Insurance Act).

§4. Pregnancy and Maternity

I. Definition

157. Neither pregnancy nor childbirth is an irregular physical condition; they are, therefore, not to be regarded as illnesses. Therefore, specific provisions have been introduced to ensure that the costs of childbirth are not imposed on women and to compensate for the loss of income caused by the ban on working for pregnant women and baby care.

II. Benefits

158. In principle, all pregnant women or mothers are entitled to the same benefits in kind, regardless of whether they are insured as employed women themselves or as family members. This also applies to wives who are already divorced if the delivery takes place within 302 days of the divorce. Cash-related benefits are, however, only available to working women (e.g., the maternity allowance).

A. General

159. All women are entitled to the following benefits in kind in connection with pregnancy and childbirth:

- assistance from doctors, midwives, qualified paediatric and infant nurses;
- remedies and medical aids; and
- institutional care for ten days.

B. Operational Assistance

160. If the women are insured under the Commercial Social Security Act and Farmers' Social Security Act, they are also entitled to operational assistance

(*Betriebshilfe*). A suitable person, trained in the area in question, shall substitute for the pregnant woman or mother in carrying out urgent tasks at the farm or enterprise.

C. Maternity Allowance

161. Employed pregnant women and those who have just given birth to a child are prohibited from working for at least eight weeks under labour law (termed mothers' protection period). During this period (eight weeks before and after birth), the maternity allowance (*Wochengeld*) is intended to provide financial support for the expectant mother and is paid as a replacement for the lost income.

162. The following are entitled to maternity allowance:

– employed women (earning more than EUR 500.91 per month; value for 2023);
– marginally employed women workers with voluntary self-insurance;
– fully insured female free employees;
– self-employed women performing a trade and female farmers if they do not make use of operating assistance as a benefit in kind; and
– self-employed women who are not performing a trade (termed the new self-employed, *Neue Selbstständige*).

163. This allowance is generally paid during the following period: eight weeks before the expected date of birth, on the day of delivery and eight weeks after delivery. The eight-week period before the expected date of delivery is calculated on the base of a medical certificate. If the delivery takes place at a time other than the time assumed by the doctor, the period before the expected date of delivery is shortened or extended accordingly. If the period of protection (and thus the payment of maternity allowance) is shortened before the birth, the period of protection (and thus the payment of maternity allowance) after the birth is generally extended accordingly, in total, to a maximum of sixteen weeks.

164. The duration of eight weeks may be increased in the following cases, however:

– In the case of multiple, premature or C-section deliveries, it may be extended to twelve weeks after birth. A premature birth is considered to be one taking place before the thirty-seventh week of pregnancy.
– If a ban on employment is imposed by gynaecologists, labour inspectors or medical officers for the period prior to the beginning of the protection period before the birth or after it.

165. The amount of the maternity allowance:

– For employed women is based on the net remuneration of the last three calendar months before the start of maternity leave. In addition, a supplement for special payments, such as holiday and Christmas bonuses, is also paid.

- Female free employees receive an income-dependent weekly allowance.
- Marginally employed persons who are self-insured (according to §19a General Social Insurance Act) receive a fixed amount of EUR 10.35 per day (value for 2023).
- Women who are self-employed and carry out a trade and female farmers also receive an allowance if they do not make use of the farm assistance in kind. In this case, the amount of the daily allowance is EUR 61.25 per day (value for 2023).
- Female recipients of unemployment insurance benefits under the Unemployment Insurance Act generally receive a weekly allowance amounting to 180% of the last benefit received.

166. Recipients of childcare allowance are only entitled to maternity allowance for an additional child if they were already entitled to maternity allowance at the time of the previous birth (i.e., for the child for which they are currently receiving childcare allowance) and only if they are entitled to childcare allowance when maternity leave begins. The amount of the maternity allowance generally represents the amount of the childcare allowance received before the birth. If a person receives an additional income while receiving maternity allowance, this may lead to a suspension of the maternity allowance equal to the income earned.

§5. Reintegration after Long-Term Sick Leave

I. Definition

167. After a long period of sick leave, employees can agree with their employer that they will reduce their working hours by 25%–50% for up to six months following this sick leave (*Wiedereingliederungsteilzeit*, part-time work to reintegrate laid down in §13 of the Employment Contract Law Adaption Act). It is intended to enable people who are in employment and who are seriously ill, physically or mentally, for a long period of time to return gently to their everyday working life. Therefore, a labour and social security law model was established, which has been in force since 1 July 2017.

168. To qualify under labour law, the employee must have been on sick leave for at least six weeks during the same employment relationship; the previous employment relationship must have lasted at least three months before the start of the reintegration of part-time work. Since the employee is considered to be absolutely fit for work during the part-time employment, a medical certificate confirming the employee's ability to work is required at the start of the part-time employment.

169. A written agreement between employer and employee about a temporary reduction of the working time is the basis of the reintegration of part-time work. Prior to this, both parties have to be advised by fit2work, a public organization that is closely connected to the labour and social security authorities. The weekly normal working time has to be reduced by at least 25% and at most 50%; however, the reduced working time must not be less than twelve hours during the reintegration part-time period, and the monthly remuneration must be above the marginal earnings threshold (2023: EUR 500.91).

II. Benefits

170. The labour regulation on reintegration after long sickness has been supplemented by benefits of social law. During part-time work, a reintegration allowance (*Wiedereingliederungsgeld*) is due to compensate for the loss of income caused by a lower level of remuneration due to the part-time agreement (§143d General Social Insurance Act).

171. The reintegration benefit is calculated on the basis of the increased sickness benefit (= 60% of the calculation base) and is proportionate to the agreed normal weekly working hours. If working time is reduced by half, the benefit is 50% of the increased sickness benefit; if one works 75% of a standard working week, one is entitled to 25% and so on.

172. While receiving a reintegration allowance, employees are not entitled to sickness allowance. If employees fall ill during the current reintegration part-time work, they continue to receive reintegration benefit instead of a sickness allowance.

173. After the end of the part-time work, the employee can only be entitled to a reintegration allowance (for a new part-time agreement) after a period of eighteen months has passed.

§6. Early Detection and Prevention of Diseases

I. Definition

174. For a long time, the primary purpose of health insurance was to provide medical assistance for ill people and to compensate for their loss of income. In the meantime, the tasks of the health insurance institutions have been extended to the area of preventive healthcare. This includes providing the population with general information on how to stay healthy and giving people the opportunity to discover possible health risks at an early stage instead of waiting for an illness to occur.

II. Benefits

175. Apart from informing the population about various health topics and educating them about accident prevention (health promotion measures), the benefits of health insurance in the area of healthcare consist, above all, of offering the insured persons the opportunity to undergo medical examinations as a precautionary measure in order to prevent the development of diseases. These precautionary examinations include, in particular:

- preventive (health) examination (§132b General Social Security Act) for insured persons and their co-insured relatives;
- health screening for adolescents for working young people.

176. In the present context, the measures to strengthen health should also be mentioned; these include, for example, recuperative stays provided by the health insurance carrier. However, this is a voluntary benefit, and the recipient has to make an additional payment (§155 General Social Insurance Act).

Part IV. Family Allowances

Chapter 1. General Information

177. The general aim of family allowances is to enable parents to provide sufficient financial means to raise and support their children; another aim is to compensate for the loss of income caused by the ban on working for pregnant women and baby care. The two most important forms of family allowances in the field of social security (in a wider sense) are the Family Benefit (*Familienbeihilfe*) and the Child Care Allowance *(Kinderbetreuungsgeld)*.

178. Both allowances are financed by tax revenues; like social welfare, they are not operated according to the insurance principle. Beneficiaries are not required to have paid contributions. As for the Family Benefit, it might be attributed even to tax law because it has to be applied for at the Tax Office (*Finanzamt*). The Family Benefit is an allowance that is granted by the Federal Fund to Compensate for Family Expenses (*Famlienlastenausgleichsfonds*), a federal institution that is also responsible for other types of family support such as free schoolbooks and traffic tickets for children, apprentices, and students. Although the Child Care Allowance is not financed by contributions, it is operated by the health insurance bodies where the beneficiaries have to apply for the benefit.

179. Additionally, there are several social insurance benefits which refer to the status of family or children. However, such benefits may be referred to as family allowances only in a wider sense because they depend on (precedent) contributions by an employed and properly insured person. Examples of insurance benefits to families are the co-insurance of children with their working parents in health insurance or family supplements in the field of cash benefits in the case of unemployment or pensions for orphans.

Chapter 2. Family Benefit

§1. Territorial and Personal Field of Application

180. The Family Benefit (*Familienbeihilfe*) is granted to all parents for their children irrespective of whether the parent is in employment or their income level (§2 Compensation for Family Expenses Act). The amount of the family benefit is governed on the basis of the number and age of the children. The allowance may be granted for an adopted child, a foster child, a stepchild or a grandchild as well.

181. Parents are entitled to family benefit if:

- the centre of their life is in Austria; and
- their child lives together with them in the same household; or
- parents and child do not live in the same household; the parents provide for the principal part of child support.

182. Therefore, also foreign nationals may be entitled to family allowances, but only if they are lawfully resident in Austria. Persons who are entitled to an equivalent foreign allowance are not entitled to Austrian family benefit.

183. After the child's eighteenth birthday, parents are entitled to family benefit for this child only under certain circumstances, especially if the child:

- is training for an occupation or studying at university; or
- will probably be permanently unable to take care of themself financially due to physical disability or psychiatric disorders, and so on.

184. In the case of severe handicaps, families may be granted the Increased Family Benefit. The requirement is that the child:

- has a disability rating of at least 50%; or
- is permanently unable to support themself.

§2. Amount of the Family Benefit

185. Family benefit is granted for each child in the family; the amount of the benefit varies according to the age of the child (§8 Compensation for Family Expenses Act; status 2023):

Age of the Child	*Monthly Amount*
From birth up to 3 years	EUR 120.61
3 years and older	EUR 129.00
10 years and older	EUR 149.70

Age of the Child	*Monthly Amount*
19 years and older	EUR 174.70
Additional supplement for a child with a severe disability	EUR 164.90

186. If there are several children in a family, the total amount of family benefit rises by the following amounts (sibling supplement scale):

Number of Children	*Monthly Amount*
for 2 children	by EUR7.50 per child
for 3 children	by EUR 18.40 per child
for 4 children	by EUR 28.00 per child
for 5 children	by EUR 33.90 per child
for 6 children	by EUR 55.00 per child

Chapter 3. Childcare Allowance

§1. Territorial and Personal Field of Application

187. The Childcare Allowance (*Kinderbetreuungsgeld*) is a cash benefit, and it is granted to families after the birth of a child up to their third birthday (at most); additionally, the beneficiaries are insured in the field of health insurance as long as they receive the allowance. Unlike the family benefit mentioned above, the childcare allowance is only granted to one child – the youngest – of the family. Furthermore, there exist strict limitations to additional income of the beneficiary during the acquisition of the allowance. In the case of the flat-rate childcare allowance, additional income may not exceed EUR 18,000.00 per year; if the parents receive the income-related childcare allowance, the additional income may not exceed EUR 7,500.00 per year.

188. There are several forms of childcare allowances depending on the coverage periods of the allowance, the economic situation of the family, and whether or not the applying parent has been employed gainfully before the child's birth. The main categories are:

- allowance in the form of a flat-rate amount;
- supplementary allowance; and
- income-related childcare allowance.

189. All parents – irrespective of any previous gainful activities – are entitled to childcare allowance for the youngest of their children in the form of a flat rate if they meet the following requirements:

- legal residence of the applying parent in Austria;
- legal residence of the child in Austria;
- parent(s) and child live in the same household;
- both parent(s) and child have valid health insurance;
- medical examinations of both mother and child as part of the mother-child programme during pregnancy and after the child's birth;– the family is entitled to Family Benefit (*Familienbeihilfe*) in Austria;
- the family is not entitled to childcare allowance from another country.

190. In the case of the income-related childcare allowance, additionally, the parent must have been gainfully employed and insured prior to the mother's protection period or the child's birth for at least 182 days.

191. Furthermore, in all cases, parents can choose whether only one or both of them receive – subsequently – the childcare allowance; in each case, only one parent is entitled to the allowance at the same time. If both parents, however, claim the allowance, in total, it is granted for a longer period. The longer periods are considered to be an additional motivation for fathers to stay at home in order to take care of the baby as well.

§2. Amount of the Childcare Allowance

I. Flat-Rate Childcare Allowance

192. The amount of childcare allowance that is granted to a family is, in total, EUR 13,085.25 if only one parent claims the allowance; the amount is EUR 16,347.60 if both parents receive – subsequently – the allowance. If only one parent receives the allowance, the daily amount of allowance, therefore, may range from EUR 15.38 (for twenty-eight months) to a maximum of EUR 35.85 per day (for twelve months). The same daily amounts are granted if both parents claim the allowance; however, then, the childcare allowances are granted for longer periods (fifteen months to thirty-five months).

193. The allowance is always granted for one child per family; however, in the event of multiple births (e.g., twins), a higher allowance is granted. Furthermore, single parents and low-income families are entitled to a supplementary allowance.

II. Income-Related Childcare Allowance

194. Parents who have been gainfully employed and insured at least 182 days prior to the date of their child's birth can apply for the income-related allowance. This variant of the childcare allowance amounts to 80% of the maternity allowance; it amounts to a maximum of EUR 69.83 per day (that is, about EUR 2,100.00 per month).

195. The maximum duration of the income-related childcare allowance is twelve months if only one parent claims the allowance and fourteen months if both parents – subsequently – receive the allowance.

Part V. Incapacity to Work

Chapter 1. General Information and Field of Application

§1. Incapacity to Work Within the Various Fields of Insurance

196. The insured event of a reduced capacity or incapacity to work is covered by several classes of social insurance in Austria. A temporary incapacity to work due to illness is mainly an insured event of health insurance; the sick employee receives medical treatment that they need to get well again (like all other sick people) and sickness allowance in order to be able to provide for their living as a surrogate for their payment. The allowance ends when the illness is over, and the employee can work again.

197. In the case of permanent incapacity, differentiation must be made between incapacities that are work-related, that is, they have been caused by work accidents or professional diseases, and other reasons for incapacity (*see* Part VI Chapter 1 §1). Additionally, the age of the incapable person is of relevance, and it plays a role in whether or not the incapable employee can work in another professional field.

§2. Permanent and Temporary Incapacity to Work

198. For insured persons covered by the General Social Insurance Act who were born in 1964 or later, the incapacity to work must be suspected to be permanent. If the incapacity to work is only temporary or can be resolved, the insured persons are entitled and obliged to seek medical or occupational rehabilitation.

199. Insured persons covered by the General Social Insurance Act who were born in 1963 or earlier and all persons insured under the Commercial Social Security Act can still claim a pension due to reduced capacity to work, even if they are only temporarily incapable of work; however, the incapacity to work must be expected to last for at least six months. In this case, the pension for reduced capacity to work will be awarded for a maximum of twenty-four months. The insured person may submit an application for continued entitlement within three months of its expiry. The time-limited nature of the plan enables the pension insurance institution to react to uncertainties in medical predictions and to new treatment options.

Chapter 2. Incapacity to Work Within the Pension Insurance Scheme

§1. General Information

200. The following section focuses on the area of incapacity to work covered by pension insurance (for general information on pension insurance, such as withdrawal of pension or child allowance, *see* Part VIII Chapter 4). The objective of the regulation is the compensation for the loss of income resulting from a reduction in earning capacity.

201. Neither the cause of the reduction in earning capacity nor the age of the insured person is relevant to the entitlement to such a pension.

202. It is only based on whether the insured person has a health impairment and, as a result, a permanently reduced earning capacity. In addition, the reduced capacity to work must not occur before the beginning of the insurance relationship. If the insured person had already been suffering from a health impairment before that date, they are not entitled to a pension. There is, however, an exception for people with disabilities who are not able to establish an earning capacity but who have already gathered 120 months of contribution (§255 section 7 General Social Insurance Act; *see also* Part IX).

203. The General Social Insurance Act, the Commercial Social Security Act and the Farmers' Social Security Act contain provisions on the insured event of reduced capacity to work; these also apply to insured persons under the General Pensions Act. A distinction between insured persons under the old and new law is only made when calculating the pension.

§2. Terminology

204. In Austrian legal terminology, different terms are still used to describe an insured event and the benefits awarded in the case of reduced capacity to work. In terms of meaning and systematic approach, however, they are all identical:

- for manual workers, the terms 'insured event of invalidity' and 'invalidity pension';
- for employees, the terms 'insured event of occupational disability' and 'occupational disability pension'; and
- for self-employed people under the Commercial Social Security Act and Farmers' Social Security Act, the terms 'insured events of incapacity to work' and 'incapacity to work pension'.

§3. ELIGIBILITY CRITERIA

I. General

205. In each case, for all insured events, the following requirements apply:

- reduction in capacity to work only occurred after the beginning of the insurance relationship;
- fulfilment of the waiting period;
- presumed permanent disability: if the pension recipient's state of health significantly improves, the disability or occupational incapacity pension can also be subsequently withdrawn (*see* Part VII, lapse of pension);
- no entitlement to reasonable, appropriate vocational rehabilitation measures;
- no entitlement to a pension benefit from the insured event of old age (with exception of the Corridor Pension); and
- the insured person must give up the activity for which he or she is considered to be disabled, unable to work or incapacitated. The insured person may pursue other activities (*see* V. Partial Pension below).

II. Waiting Period

206. The waiting period means that a certain number of insurance months must be completed within a specified period (regarding the old law, *see* also Part VIII Chapter 1 §2). The perpetual entitlement for reduced capacity to work is generally fulfilled if the insured person has accumulated a total of 180 contribution months (= 15 years with a maximum of 12 self-insurance months) or 300 insurance months (= 25 years). Alternatively, the waiting period for reduced capacity to work is fulfilled if 60 insurance months (= 5 years) have been completed within the last 120 calendar months (= 10 years) prior to the relevant date. If the date of reference happens to be after the age of 50, the conditions are tightened in order to prevent older insured persons from fleeing into a disability or occupational disability pension.

207. On the other hand, access to the invalidity or occupational disability pension is made easier for young insured persons. Up to the age of 27, the waiting period is already fulfilled with 6 insurance months. In any case, the waiting period is fulfilled if the insured person has acquired 180 insurance months during his or her working career.

208. In addition, the insured person is required to undergo reasonable medical treatment before claiming benefits under the pension insurance. They have an obligation to cooperate. If the insured person refuses to undergo medical treatment, they lose their pension entitlement for the period of refusal.

III. Rehabilitation Before Retirement

209. The pension for reduced earning capacity is intended to compensate for loss of income due to health-related reduction in earning capacity; however, if there is the possibility of improving the insured person's state of health to such an extent that he or she can be fit for work again, this option should be preferred. That is, in principle, 'rehabilitation before retirement'.

210. Therefore, according to §361 section 1 General Social Insurance Act, an application by the insured person for an invalidity, occupational or disability pension is, at the same time, to be considered as an application for rehabilitation measures. The insured person does not have to agree to the rehabilitation measures.

211. Among the rehabilitation measures, a distinction must be made between medical and occupational measures.

212. The objective of medical rehabilitation measures is to improve the insured person's state of health to such an extent that he or she can resume his or her previous occupation or an occupation of a referral profession. Only when medical rehabilitation measures do not promise an improvement is a permanent disability or occupational or earning incapacity recognized.

213. Occupational rehabilitation measures are, in principle, specifically for insured persons with occupational protection; however, such rehabilitation measures can also be taken if the insured person has acquired either:

- at least 12 insurance months within the last 36 calendar months before the reference date; or
- at least 36 insurance months within the last 180 calendar months before the reference date.

214. The occupational rehabilitation measures include retraining measures in particular. This is intended to reduce or prevent the incapacity to work and, with a high probability, to enable a long-term reintegration into the labour market. A retraining measure should take place with reference to the labour market and must be reasonable for the insured person.

215. The mental and physical condition of the insured person, their previous employment and training, state of health and age must be taken into account for the assessment of reasonableness. In addition, the duration, costs and scope of the training proposed also play a role. If the retraining leads to a professional activity that is significantly below the previous qualification level, the insured must also agree to the measure.

216. The pension insurance institution decides whether an entitlement to occupational measures exists and for which occupational field the insured person should be rehabilitated. The occupational rehabilitation measures are implemented by the

Labour Market Service (*Arbeitsmarktservice*). The Labour Market Service, formerly known as the Labour Office (until 1993), is the most important institution in the area of unemployment insurance and state labour market policy.

217. As long as occupational rehabilitation measures are reasonable, the insured person is not entitled to a pension due to reduced capacity to work.

218. The insured person is entitled to benefits in cash for the duration of the rehabilitation measures. For the duration of medical rehabilitation measures, the insured person receives rehabilitation benefits (*Rehabilitationsgeld*) from health insurance. If an occupational rehabilitation measure is carried out, the insured person is entitled to retraining benefits (*Umschulungsgeld*) from unemployment insurance benefits.

IV. Determination of the Incapacity to Work

219. As part of the procedure for a pension application, the pension insurance institution checks whether all the conditions for the pension are met. The 'Competence Centre Assessment' decides on the insured person's capacity for both employment and rehabilitation.

220. The health impairment of the insured person and their performance is evaluated on the basis of medical reports. By way of such a medical performance assessment (*medizinisches Leistungskalkül*), an expert provides information in an expert opinion on which referral professions can be assigned to the insured, taking into account the medical assessment which, combined, constitutes the 'occupational performance assessment' (*berufliches Leistungskalkül*). In addition, the expert will state whether and which retraining measures are appropriate.

221. Expected sickness rates are also taken into account when assessing the incapacity to work. Case law regularly assumes that people who are on sick leave for six to seven weeks per year are incapable of work. Personal circumstances, such as lack of language skills or care obligations towards children or relatives, are not considered.

222. If labour market-related issues need to be clarified, an experienced representative of the Labour Market Service can also be called in.

223. If the pension insurance institution rejects the pension application because of a lack of permanent incapacity to work, it still has to make certain clarifications, including whether invalidity or occupational disability has occurred, whether it is expected to last six months, whether occupational rehabilitation measures are appropriate and reasonable and if so, for which occupational field, and whether there is an entitlement to rehabilitation benefit (§367 section 4 General Social Insurance Act).

224. If the pension insurance institution rejects the application with a decision, the applicant can proceed against the decision, initiating a social court proceeding. In these social court proceedings, court-certified experts will again estimate the professional and medical performance. Finally, the court rules on whether the referral occupation can be considered reasonable for the insured person.

225. In order to avoid too many lawsuits, a waiting period must be observed in the event of the dismissal of an action (§362 General Social Insurance Act); accordingly, a new pension application may only be made within the next eighteen months if there is a significant change in the previously determined incapacity to work. A reduction of at least 10% is deemed to be substantial.

§4. Benefits

I. Invalidity Pension

226. The term 'invalidity pension' refers to the pension from the insured event of reduced working capacity for workers. Initially, a distinction must be made between the following groups of persons when assessing whether a worker is disabled:

- workers in a skilled occupation or profession (skilled or semi-skilled workers); and
- workers who are unskilled (unskilled workers).

227. Workers are to be considered skilled workers if they have successfully completed prescribed training courses, such as the successful completion of an apprenticeship according to the Vocational Training Act. If the insured person has learned several occupations, then it must be determined whether they can still be active in one of these occupations; only if this is not the case is the insured person considered to be disabled.

228. Semi-skilled workers are those workers who carry out an activity which requires the acquisition of qualified knowledge or skills through practical work. This knowledge shall be equivalent to that acquired in a trained occupation. Semi-skilled workers shall be treated in the same way as skilled workers.

229. Unskilled, however, are all workers who have been neither trained nor taught.

A. Invalidity of Skilled and Semi-Skilled Workers

230. According to §255 section 1 General Social Insurance Act, skilled and semi-skilled workers are considered to have an invalidity if:

- their capacity to work has been reduced to less than half of the working capacity of a physically and mentally healthy insured person of similar education and equivalent knowledge and skills in each of these occupations; and
- this is due to their physical or mental condition.

231. The insured person must have worked in trained or semi-skilled occupations for the most part. This means that the insured person must have worked in the trained or semi-skilled profession for at least 90 insurance months (= 7.5 insurance years) during the last 15 years before the date of reference. This requirement is particularly difficult to meet for the long-term unemployed. They are, therefore, often regarded as unskilled, even though they have practised their trained profession throughout the time they have been employed.

232. Trained and semi-skilled workers enjoy occupational protection (*Berufsschutz*). This means that insured persons do not have to carry out any other activity before they are awarded an invalidity pension. They only have to work in their previous occupation and referral occupations, which are closely connected (*Verweisungsberufe*), respectively.

233. A referral profession is a profession which requires similar training and the acquisition of similar skills and knowledge as the profession previously practised. The referral profession must still exist in Austria; in other words, there must be at least one hundred jobs; it is irrelevant, however, whether these jobs are vacant.

234. In summary, a skilled or semi-skilled worker is regarded as an invalid if, because of his or her poor health, he or she is unable to carry out even half of his or her previous job or a referral job. If the person can be expected to exercise a referral profession, the person is not considered an invalid. Whether they actually find employment in the referral profession is not decisive. The fact that the insured person may not find employment is a risk covered by unemployment insurance.

235. The insured person's capacity to work is reduced by half only if the worker in the referral occupation earns less than half the average wage of a healthy worker in that occupation.

B. Invalidity of Unskilled Workers

236. For unskilled workers, the requirements for receiving an invalidity pension are much stricter (§255 section 3 General Social Insurance Act). In fact, unskilled workers do not benefit from any occupational protection. This means that an unskilled worker is only awarded an invalidity pension if he or she can no longer perform any employment in which he or she earns at least half of the remuneration that a healthy insured person regularly earns through such employment.

237. An unskilled worker at the age of 50 or more is considered to be incapable of work if he or she was unemployed for at least twelve months immediately prior to the reference date, has completed at least thirty years of insurance, including at least twenty years of contributions due to employment, can only perform activities with a low requirement profile and is not to be expected to be able to obtain a corresponding job within one year (§255 section 3a and 3b General Social Insurance Act). Colloquially, this regulation is called a hardship provision (*Härtefallregelung*).

238. Additionally, according to the professional skills protection laid down in §255 section 4 General Social Insurance Act, an unskilled worker at the age of 60 or more is considered to be incapable of work if they cannot perform an activity that they have carried out for at least ten years during the last fifteen years prior to the reference date (*Tätigkeitsschutz*).

II. Occupational Disability Pension

239. The term 'occupational disability pension' (*Berufsunfähigkeitspension*) refers to the pension from insured event of reduced capacity to work for salaried employees. The eligibility criteria that must be met for an employee to be entitled to an occupational disability pension are identical to those for an invalidity pension. Only the term 'occupational disability' is defined differently.

240. Employees generally benefit from occupational protection for the profession they have exercised for at least 7.5 years in the last 15 years prior to the reference date. Employees who have not practised a particular profession for the above-mentioned minimum period do not enjoy occupational protection. In that case, they are to be treated in the same way as unskilled workers.

241. The profession that an employee can reasonably be expected to carry out before he or she is entitled to an occupational disability pension depends on the applicable collective agreement. The collective agreement divides employees into groups depending on the job requirements and qualifications. The classification is also important for remuneration. An activity within the same category is reasonable in any case. According to case law, an activity belonging to a lower category is also acceptable (the protection for employees 60 years or older is the same as for workers). Only if the employee cannot be reasonably expected to perform any of these activities does occupational protection apply, and the required employee's occupational disability is given.

III. Incapacity to Work Pension

242. The term 'incapacity to work pension' (*Invaliditätspension*) refers to the pension from the insured event of reduced capacity to work for self-employed persons obligatorily insured under the Commercial Social Security Act or Farmers' Social Security Act.

243. Like unskilled workers, self-employed persons do not enjoy occupational protection. They are not considered to be incapacitated until they are no longer able to pursue any regular occupation.

244. There are three possible exceptions to this rule; however, all of them depend on age. Structurally, they are very similar to the above-described hardship provisions designed for employed persons:

(1) From the age of 50: self-employed persons whose work is necessary to keep the business running enjoy occupational protection. They can only be referred to as self-employed activities which require similar training and equivalent skills to the occupation they last performed for at least five years (§133 section 2 Commercial Social Security Act).
(2) From the age of 50: a self-employed person is considered to be incapable of work if they have been unemployed for at least twelve months immediately prior to the reference date, have completed a not inconsiderable waiting period (= at least thirty years of insurance, including at least twenty years of contributions due to employment), can only perform activities with a low requirement profile and are not to be expected to be able to obtain a corresponding job within one year (§133 section 2a and 2b Commercial Social Security Act as well as §124 section 1a and 2b Farmers' Social Security Act; similar to the provisions applicable to unskilled workers).
(3) From the age of 60: like workers and employees, the self-employed also enjoy protection for those activities which they have carried out for at least ten years during the last fifteen years prior to the reference date. A special condition applying to the self-employed is that a reasonable change in the equipment and staffing of their business must be taken into account (§133 section 3 Commercial Social Security Act as well as §124 section 2 Farmers' Social Security Act).

IV. Pension Amount

245. The calculation of the pension due to incapacity for work is based on the total balance credited to one's pension account. The pension account is designed for retirement pension purposes and is based on insurance periods. If insurance periods are missing due to incapacity to work, the total credit might be unreasonably low. In these cases, the total credit is then multiplied by a certain factor (for details, *see* §§5 and 6 General Pensions Act).

246. Under the old legislation, the calculation of the pension due to incapacity for work for insured persons follows the calculation of the old-age pension (*see* also Part VIII Chapter 1 §2). Missing insurance periods must be compensated for. For this reason, from the reference date up to the age of 60, additional insurance months are added. The increased amount is then reduced again by a deduction (maximum 13.8%) and may not exceed 60%.

V. Partial Pension

247. An insured person receiving a pension for incapacity to work may, in principle, engage in an occupational activity; however, this must not be the occupation for which the insured person is disabled or unable to work. If the additional income exceeds the marginal earnings threshold, the entitlement to a pension for incapacity to work is converted into an entitlement to partial pension. This means that the entitlement to a pension due to incapacity to work is reduced if the total monthly income (= pension due to incapacity to work + earned income) exceeds EUR 1,357.72 (as of 2023).

VI. In Relation to the Regular Retirement Pension

248. After reaching the statutory retirement age, the insured person receiving a pension due to their incapacity to work can submit an application for a regular retirement pension. In other words, the conversion of the work incapacity pension into an old-age pension is not carried out automatically but upon request.

Part VI. Industrial Accidents and Occupational Diseases

Chapter 1. (General and) Field of Application

§1. General Information

249. In Austria, industrial accidents and occupational diseases represent the two most relevant insured events covered by the accident insurance scheme. The purpose of an accident insurance policy is to cover or compensate for the risk of personal injury to an employee resulting from his or her employment. Historically, this type of insurance – along with health insurance – is one of the oldest classes of insurance. Without such an accident insurance scheme, the damaged employee would have to claim damages directly against the employer on the basis of general tort law according to the General Civil Code. In doing so, the employee would have to bear the full risk of litigation and costs; in addition, it might have a negative effect on the working climate.

250. The concept of the Austrian accident insurance scheme is that only the employer pays into the accident insurance scheme (1.2% of the contribution base or payroll total) while the risk of personal injury to his employees resulting from the employment is transferred to the accident insurance scheme. In other words, employers 'buy themselves out' and – with a few exceptions – are not liable for damages to their employees. The employees claim damages against the accident insurance institution as a neutral body; this also prevents the damaged employee from having to claim damages from an insolvent injuring party.

251. The main objectives of the accident insurance scheme are to restore the employee's health as well as their ability to work and to participate in society. The impairment of health should be eliminated, that is, healed, or at least, a further impairment should be prevented. Permanent occupational disability should be prevented. The aim of cash benefits is compensation for loss of income due to (partial) incapacity to work.

252. In the field of accident insurance, there are two insurance cases: industrial accident (§§175 et seq. General Social Insurance Act) and occupational disease (§177 and Annex 1 to the General Social Insurance Act). For employees and free employees (full insurance according to §4 General Social Insurance Act) as well as self-employed persons (partial insurance in the accident insurance according to §8 section 1 No. 3 General Social Insurance Act), the regulations of the General Social Insurance Act apply. Parallel regulations were essentially adopted for civil servants (§§90, 91 Civil Servants Health and Accident Insurance Act) on industrial accidents, and §92 Civil Servants Health and Accident Insurance Act with reference to Annex 1 to the General Social Insurance Act on occupational diseases). Proper regulations apply to farmers and foresters (scope of application §3 Farmers' Social Security Act); industrial accidents §148c, §148d Farmers' Social Security Act; occupational disease §148e Farmers' Social Security Act, also with reference to Annex 1 to the General Social Insurance Act).

253. Over time, areas beyond mere gainful employment have been included in accident insurance coverage, such as accidents during training on the job, participation in workplace democracy or during labour market service measures. Furthermore, even accidents or diseases which have no connection with one's employment may constitute an accident insurance case: if someone saves another's life, for example, on the occasion of a car crash and gets hurt on this occasion, this constitutes a professional accident. The same applies to diseases a person contracts as a result of donating blood.

§2. Personal Scope of Application and the Accident Insurance Institutions

254. All insured persons, that is to say, all gainfully employed persons, pupils and students, as well as – in the event of death of the insured person – certain relatives, are entitled to benefits under the accident insurance.

I. Insured Workforce

255. This group includes:

- employees according to §4 section 2 General Social Insurance Act;
- free employees (*freie Dienstnehmer*; also known as quasi-employees) according to §4 section 4 General Social Insurance Act;
- 'old' and 'new' self-employed persons (*Alte und Neue Selbstständige*) according to the Commercial Social Security Act and farmers as well as foresters according to the Farmers' Social Security Act; and
- members of the professions (*Angehörige der freien Berufe*).

II. Insured Kindergarten Children, Pupils and Students

256. Children and young people at various stages of education are also insured. In contrast to health insurance, where this group is included in their parent's insurance, they are explicitly covered by the insurance on their own; however, kindergarten children, schoolchildren and students do not have to make any contributions.

257. Insured are:

- kindergarten children in their last year before starting compulsory school (§8 section 1 No. 3 lit l General Social Insurance Act);
- pupils in compulsory general education, vocational schools and academies as well as secondary general education (§8 section 1 No 3 lit h, §175 sections 4 and 5 General Social Insurance Act); and
- students undergoing teaching and education training at institutions: in universities, art colleges and theological colleges or at universities of applied sciences. (§8 section 1 No. 3 lit l, §175 sections 4 and 5 General Social Insurance Act).

258. In the case of schoolchildren and kindergarten children, citizenship is not relevant; however, students are only insured against accidents if they are either Austrian citizens, citizens of a European Economic Area (EEA) state or citizens of a country with which a social security agreement (including accident insurance) exists.

III. Accident Insurance Institutions for Each Protected Group

259. The accidental insurance institutions for each protected group are indicated as follows:

Austrian Social Insurance for Occupational Risks (Allgemeine Unfallversicherungsanstalt – AUVA)	*Insurance Institution for Public Servants, Railways and Mining (Versicherungsanstalt öffentlich Bediensteter, Eisenbahnen und Bergbau – BVAEB)*	*Social Insurance Institution of the Self-employed (Sozialversicherungsanstalt der Selbständigen – SVS)*
– Blue-collar and white-collar workers. – Kindergarten children during their compulsory kindergarten year. – School pupils and students. – Other persons protected in the event of damage (e.g., lifesavers).	– Tenured civil servants at federal, state and local levels. – Federal contract staff employed from 1 January 1999. – Railway and mining employees. – Staff of cableway installations.	– Self-employed persons in agriculture and forestry as well as their relatives. – Self-employed persons with or without trade licenses.

Austrian Social Insurance for Occupational Risks (Allgemeine Unfallversicherungsanstalt – AUVA)	*Insurance Institution for Public Servants, Railways and Mining (Versicherungsanstalt öffentlich Bediensteter, Eisenbahnen und Bergbau – BVAEB)*	*Social Insurance Institution of the Self-employed (Sozialversicherungsanstalt der Selbständigen – SVS)*
	– Staff of sleeping and dining car operations. – Certain employees of the Austrian Railway Company (*ÖBB*). – Certain employees of the public transit network (*Wiener Linien*).	

Chapter 2. Insured Events and the Reduced Capacity to Work

§1. CONCEPT OF INDUSTRIAL ACCIDENT

I. Legal Definition and Criteria

260. According to §175 General Social Insurance Act, an industrial accident (*Arbeitsunfall*) is an accident that is locally, temporally and causally related to employment (in the following, for other groups *see* §§148c and 148d Farmers' Social Security Act, §§90 and 91 Civil Servants Health and Accident Insurance Law, referred to therein as *Dienstunfall*, only the relevant regulations of the General Social Insurance Act are referred to).

261. A legal definition of the term 'accident' is not given by law. According to the doctrine, accidents are understood to be events coming from the outside and suddenly occurring or limited in time, which have an effect on the body or psyche of the employee and lead to a personal injury. Furthermore, the event may involve a behaviour of the injured person that deviates from the routine or involves extraordinary stress. Accident insurance does not, therefore, cover property damages or financial losses. It is irrelevant, however, at what point in time the health disorder occurs as a result of the accident; the damage may only become evident a long time after the accident.

II. Protected Situations

262. Furthermore, the accident must have occurred under certain circumstances, termed protected area of life (*geschützter Lebensbereich*); these activities may not involve self-economic activities. The self-economic, in other words, private, area includes, above all, the necessary and self-evident things which every person habitually does independently of his or her professional activity (e.g., sleeping, eating, washing, changing personal laundry). If a certain activity carried out by the insured person (also during working hours) is determined solely or predominantly by self-economic purposes, there is no operational connection for the duration of this activity (e.g., buying groceries during on-call duty; snowboarding by an apprentice waiter during on-call duty; painting the former office space which the employer provides for the employee to live in; expert legal advice to an employee at the Labour Market Service on their own initiative).

263. The accident which led to personal injury must, therefore, have occurred during employment or while attending an educational establishment (kindergarten, school or university), or the damaging activity must have been an act in the interest of another person or the community.

264. In addition to those activities within the scope of the employment contract, the legislator has included other activities in the scope of protection which are more or less closely related to the employment activity. Besides the general clause (§175 section 1 General Social Insurance Act), therefore, the General Social Insurance Act also contains clarifying and expanding rules for classification as an industrial accident in order to achieve the broadest possible inclusion. In addition to accidents whose cause results 'directly' from the insured occupation, §175 section 2 General Social Insurance Act expressly considers various accidents while travelling to and from work to be occupational accidents. Other accidents – even if they are not related to employment – are also regarded as industrial accidents according to §176 section 1 General Social Insurance Act (including the rescue of a person from the risk of death).

265. In summary, this means that if the damage to health has occurred in the course of a predominantly self-economic activity, it is not protected in terms of accident insurance since the connection with his or her gainful employment or with certain actions in the general interest no longer exists.

A. Accident during Employment

266. The accident must have occurred during employment; this basically includes all activities which the employee carries out in fulfilment of their contractual obligations, including any additional or more specific instructions by his or her employer or superior (§175 section 1 No. 3 General Social Insurance Act).

267. For this reason, the accident scheme primarily covers risks to which an insured person is exposed as an employed person. The behaviour during which the accident occurs must appear to be part of his or her gainful employment (*objective condition*). Actions which are usually, and with a reasonable understanding of the respective job, still must be recognized as a professional activity must be taken into account. Furthermore, the activity must be performed with the intention of currently performing the gainful employment (*subjective condition*). In principle, it is sufficient if the employee – from his or her point of view – thinks that the activity is suitable to serve the interests of the company.

268. The employee's own economic activity may also be protected in the event of special circumstances arising from the company's activities (e.g., drinking during physically demanding work), however, or even if the self-employed activity serves to maintain or restore the ability to work (tram driver taking a shower on a midsummer's day; body cleansing after contact with harmful substances or after extreme pollution at work).

269. Industrial accidents during employment can also occur during the storage, maintenance, testing, transport and renewal of work equipment (§175 section 2 No. 5 General Social Insurance Act); however, work equipment within the meaning of this provision can only be referred to if it is used primarily for operational purposes: for instance, the assistance of a colleague in starting up a vehicle used for operational purposes is protected.

B. Business Trips

270. Business trips are services performed by an employee outside his usual workplace or the company headquarters. These may be trips to customers as well as attending conferences and trade fairs or, furthermore, professional training events. During such trips and company-related training events, it is particularly difficult to distinguish between working hours, breaks and free time and between business and private activities. As a rule, business travellers have to satisfy their vital needs under different conditions to those when working at their place of employment. For this reason, a participant in a training course also benefits from accident insurance protection when leaving or going back to the location of training or his accommodation in order to satisfy his or her vital needs, in particular, to eat meals together with the course participants. The protection does not apply, however, if the traveller carries out personal activities which are no longer significantly influenced by the business activity (e.g., going to the bathroom or visiting a restaurant after the end of business activities; according to the case law, however, there was a sufficient connection to the business activity in the case of participation in obligatory shooting exercises as an accompanying programme or in the case of a dog bite during a break under a shady tree due to excessively hot training rooms).

C. Commuting Accidents

271. According to §175 section 2 No. 1 General Social Insurance Act, an accident on the journey ‘to or from the place of work’ explicitly constitutes an industrial accident (*Wegunfall*). This includes the route between the place of work and permanent residence (and *vice versa*). As a requirement, there must also be a local, temporal and causal (internal) connection between the distance travelled and the operational activity.

272. This internal connection would be missing if the accident occurred on the way to work but was caused by a hazard within the private sphere (e.g., a fall caused by a dog belonging to another person due to taking along their own dog). If, however, special conditions at work or on the way to and from work favour such a damaging event, a robbery for personal motives or an accident due to microsleep or intoxication may even be covered.

273. In principle, the way to work begins or ends outside one’s home, that is to say, when one passes through the entrance door of one’s apartment building. According to regulations introduced by the Act on Measures against COVID-19, accidents that occur in a temporal and causal connection with employment at the insured person’s place of residence (*home office*) are also considered to be industrial accidents according to §175 section 1a and 1b General Social Insurance Act.

274. As a rule, the house or garage door leading to the outside can be regarded as the relevant distinguishing feature. That is why slipping just inside the house is no longer covered. In mixed-use buildings or apartments, however, an internal staircase may still be covered by the protection zone if it leads to the (employee's own) business or work premises. The same applies in the case of working at the employee's home (telework in the home office) based on a home office agreement.

275. The 'permanent place of residence or stay' is where the insured person actually stays frequently and regularly (his or her centre of life). Moreover, since an employee's permanent residence might be too far away from their workplace and, therefore, they reside at a secondary residence, the way from and to the secondary residences enjoys explicit protection (§175 section 2 No. 1 2nd half-sentence General Social Insurance Act); however, the insurance coverage for the journey home of a Turkish worker to his family, which took place once a year, and for a worker who visited his family in Former Yugoslavia twice a month was denied. The way from and to secondary residences that are only used temporarily, for example, for recreational purposes, are also not protected. If the insured person is temporarily prevented from living in their home by objective circumstances, however, the routes between their place of work and his alternative accommodation are also protected by the insurance; the route between the temporary residence and external training (e.g., overnight accommodation with a course colleague for learning purposes) is also covered.

276. In principle, only the direct route between the place of residence and the place of work (or, in the case of a business trip, also between any other starting point or destination of a journey) is covered by the accident insurance scheme. If the insured person can use several possible routes for their (home) journey, they must always choose the shortest route; however, in the case of car-pooling, detours caused by the different places of residence of the participants are protected (§175 section 2 No. 9 General Social Insurance Act).

277. Short breaks in the journey home (up to two hours) do not automatically mean that there is no longer any internal connection between these journeys and the business activity; however, journeys which serve the employee's own economic interests (e.g., shopping trips) are not covered by insurance, nor is a longer interruption of the journey home at the sausage stand after the employee has been sent home early by his employer because of intoxication. Only the continuation of the journey home after a (relatively short) interruption restores the connection with the employment.

D. Other Protected Routes

278. Furthermore, the routes to and from nurseries, kindergartens, schools and other training or care facilities, such as 'daycare' or 'external care' in general, in order to bring or pick up one's (own or 'entrusted') children before or after work, are explicitly covered by accident insurance law (§175 section 2 No. 10 General Social Insurance Act; not, however, a visit to one's sick son at home during working hours). Employees on their way to or from medical treatment (e.g., in a doctor's office or ambulance) are also protected if the employer has been notified of the visit to the medical institution (§175 section 2 No. 2 General Social Insurance Act; however, there is no protection for the way to a medical examination at the social insurance institution in order to obtain approval for a stay at a health resort). Despite the fact that it is now possible to transfer money via the Internet or withdraw it regardless of bank opening hours, the 'first' bank transfer to or from 'withdrawal of the non-cash transfer' in one month is also protected (§175 section 2 No. 8 General Social Insurance Act). It cannot be repeated as often as desired; however, later journeys of the employee to the financial institution during the same month are no longer considered to be covered.

279. According to §175 section 2 No. 7 General Social Insurance Act, however, accidents that occur during working hours or during breaks at the workplace or in his or her home on the way to and also from the place of work in order to satisfy 'vital personal needs' are also classified as industrial accidents (i.e., in particular, to take meals or to go to the bathroom); however, insurance cover is only provided for needs that cannot be postponed. Consequently, the purchase of food is not subject to the provision.

E. Social Events Organized by the Company

280. For damage that occurs at social celebrations such as employees' birthdays, company Christmas parties, joint excursions, or sports events to be considered a professional accident, the party or event has to be (at least partially) financed and initiated by the employer, and it has to serve to promote community spirit and team spirit. It must be established that the majority of employees actually take part in such events.

281. For company celebrations, however, the insurance only covers the 'official part' of the celebration and the journey home right afterwards (e.g., a working lunch with superiors or the participation of a works council member, including a speech, at a privately organized retirement celebration); a subsequent 'leisurely part' lasting a further three hours is not covered, nor are group visits by the boss with his staff after work or the celebration of a promotion in a smaller setting.

282. Sports activities on works outings that exceed the usual risk associated with such events are not covered by accident insurance unless the participants, due to the nature of their profession, possess special qualifications for the practice of such an activity. According to case law, activities of 'risky marginal sports' such as rafting or canyoning, skiing or horseback riding, which are undertaken during a works outing, can also be covered by the scope of protection if the participants have the relevant prior knowledge and the activity is an obligatory part of a joint company event without having a competitive character; however, it should be noted that less athletic employees may possibly be excluded from such events. In these cases, the necessary 'care of solidarity' might not be guaranteed due to the lack of a corresponding number of participants, and consequently, accidents might not be covered. Even participation in (international or athletic) competitions may be covered by the accident insurance if it is, at least loosely – for example, for advertising or image cultivation – related to the insured (non-sporting) activity (e.g., instructed participation in the European police skiing championships). The participation of employees in group events (company parties, company outings, etc.) is covered by accident insurance (only) as long as it arises from the employment activity.

F. Activities Related to Works Constitution Law

283. Activities related to Works Organization Law include both activities as a member of an employee representative body (works council meeting, negotiations on a company agreement with the employer or company visit) and the employee who goes to a staff meeting. Accidents that happen on the occasion of such activities are, therefore, considered to be accidents at work.

G. Actions of General Interest

284. In some cases, the activities during which the equivalent workplace accidents occur are at least (to some extent) still related to employment. In other cases, however, the protected activities must be described as 'unrelated to the workplace' (*betriebsfern*). The latter group includes, in particular, accidents during the rescue of any person in danger of his or her life or during blood donation (§176 section 1 No. 2 General Social Insurance Act). In addition, this also includes accidents occurring while working as a member of an aid organization as well as (voluntary) work for aid organizations such as the voluntary fire brigade, Red Cross, mountain rescue, etc. (§176 section 1 No. 7 lit a General Social Insurance Act). For these activities, it is not the connection to gainful employment that is the decisive reason for inclusion in accident insurance, but one's altruistic action, which is to be rewarded and safeguarded for the general public.

H. Kindergarten Children, Pupils and Students

285. In addition to accidents that occur at kindergarten, school or university, accidents that are related to education, such as participation in excursions, ski courses, school weeks and statutory vocational orientation, as well as accidents on the way to kindergarten, school or university or on the way home from there, also fall within the protected area of life. Insurance coverage is also provided when exercising a compulsory or usual practical activity within the framework of the curriculum or the study regulations.

III. Imputability

286. It must be determined whether the activity causing the damage falls only within the protected area or whether the activity also involves self-economic activities, that is to say, whether private interests have also been carried out (so-termed mixed activities or mixed cases). In these cases, the insurance protection does also apply to such activities if the following three conditions are met.

A. *Condition of Causality*

287. First of all, it has to be determined whether the damaging event was the cause of the employee's personal injury. For this purpose, the *conditio sine qua non* formula applies: if the event causing the damage can be disregarded and the personal injury also ceases to exist, the event was causal in relation to the damage.

B. *Condition of Meaning: Adequacy*

288. This condition determines whether a sufficient, significant and adequate link or a substantive connection can be established between the harmful event and the employment. If the employee of a financial institution is attacked during a walk in the park at the weekend by a former customer to whom he or she has refused a loan, a connection in terms of content does exist.

C. *Theory of the Essential Condition or Essential Contributing Cause*

289. The purpose of this condition is, again, to attribute activities that have both private and professional components. The question is whether the occupational causes or those from the private sphere were essential in causing the damage. If the outcome had occurred at a much later point in time or only to a lesser extent, it would not have represented a significant contributing cause.

290. An example is the predisposition damages (*Anlageschäden*): in this case, the employee already has an illness, and then an accident occurs during work (e.g., a heart attack). An examination is made to determine whether the bodily injury occurred significantly earlier due to the work or whether it would have occurred independently of the work performed during this time.

291. Another example concerns the 'occasional' causes (*Gelegenheitsursachen*): 'mixed activities' are usually protected if they are also intended to serve business interests to a considerable extent (e.g., visiting a restaurant to have a business meeting). Cases where professional interests take such a back seat to private interests that they can only be considered an 'occasional cause' for performing the activity are not covered, however. This is the case if the injury would also have occurred through another everyday event or at about the same time, even without the accident happening. The decisive factor is that the activity performed (on the employer's instructions) must serve third-party economic interests (e.g., trying out the employer's motorcycle during lunch break) and is not predominantly determined by the insured person's own interests, such as taking the employer's motorcycle for a joy-ride in his or her leisure time.

§2. Concept of Occupational Disease

292. If the employee's health impairments are caused by stress or effects associated with the job, an occupational disease (*Berufskrankheit*) may be present. The occupational disease is a specific legal term in the General Social Insurance Act. In contrast to the narrower concept of illness according to §120 General Social Insurance Act (§80 Commercial Social Security Act, §76 Farmers' Social Security Act, §53 Civil Servants Health and Accident Insurance Law), the concept of 'occupational disease' does not always require the possibility of positive treatment. In principle, the law distinguishes between abstract and concrete occupational diseases (§177 General Social Insurance Act, §148e Farmers' Social Security Act, §92 Civil Servants Health and Accident Insurance Law).

293. According to §177 section 1 General Social Insurance Act, Annex 1 to the General Social Insurance Act provides a list of so-termed abstract occupational diseases, including their respective criteria (*see also* §148e section 1 Farmers' Social Security Act, §92 sections 1 and 2 Civil Servants Health and Accident Insurance Law also with reference to the Annex 1 to the General Social Insurance Act). If an employee has a disease listed in that register and is employed by a business referred to in the register, the disease is regarded as an occupational disease without the employee having to provide any further proof (e.g., catching an infectious disease in a hospital, Borreliosis in an agricultural holding or cataract disease in a glass manufacturing company). With a few exceptions, the occupational diseases explicitly described are mainly relevant to manual workers who are very often exposed to pollutants or noise and vibration. Mental illnesses such as burn-out are not to be found on the list; occupational illnesses can also be caused by infections with bacteria or viruses. The most common occupational diseases are hearing loss, skin diseases and respiratory diseases.

294. If an occupational disease is not listed in Annex 1 to the General Social Insurance Act, it can be considered a concrete occupational disease in individual cases under the following conditions (§177 section 2 General Social Insurance Act, §148e section 2 Farmers' Social Security Act, §92 section 3 Civil Servants Health and Accident Insurance Law):

- A determination by the accident insurance institutions on the basis of scientific evidence that the disease has, exclusively or predominantly, been caused by the use of harmful substances or radiation in the course of an occupation carried out by the insured person.

– In addition, the competent federal minister must give his consent to the determination for each individual case.

295. The regulation on concrete occupational disease serves to avoid hardship cases. It should also be possible in individual cases to receive accident insurance benefits if there is a physical impairment which is not an illness covered by Annex 1 to the General Social Insurance Act or which occurs in a company not specifically mentioned therein.

296. As a result, it is usually easier for the affected employees to claim an abstract occupational disease; furthermore, there are differences in benefits depending on the type of occupational disease.

Chapter 3. Benefits

§1. General

297. As regards accident insurance benefits, there are two main types of benefits: benefits in kind and cash benefits. In addition, the type of benefit depends on whether the employee is temporarily or permanently incapacitated for work or whether the employee has died as a result of an accident at work or occupational disease. If an employee's death is the result of an industrial accident or occupational disease, survivors' benefits are provided. These include survivors' pensions and partial reimbursement of funeral expenses. In the case of incapacity to work resulting from the insured events, a disability pension is due.

298. The benefits in kind include medical accident treatment, rehabilitation, and the provision of medical kits. The cash benefits comprise integrity compensation, family allowance and daily allowance, as well as the disability pension and allowance, and also the various forms of pensions for surviving family members. The amount of the cash benefits is mainly based on the employee's previous earnings and the extent of incapacity to work.

299. One of the main objectives of these benefits granted under the accident insurance scheme is to improve or eliminate the health disorder or reduction in earning capacity caused by an industrial accident or occupational disease or to prevent a worsening of the condition by appropriate means (§189 section 1 General Social Insurance Act, §148p section 1 Farmers' Social Security Act, §96 section 1 Civil Servants Health and Accident Insurance Law). Another objective is the compensation for the loss of income due to work accidents and professional illnesses.

300. In addition to the presence of an industrial accident or an occupational disease, the extent of the reduction in earning capacity, that is to say, the extent to which the working capacity of the affected employee is impaired, is of central importance.

§2. Benefits in Kind: Various Forms of Medical Care

301. Benefits in kind include accident treatment and rehabilitation as well as medical aids.

I. Accident Treatment

302. As a rule, accident treatment (*Unfallheilbehandlung*) is to be provided for an unlimited period of time; in any case, at least as long and as often as necessary until the state of health has been improved, a worsening of the situation can be prevented, or the ability to work is restored (§190 General Social Insurance Act, §148q Farmers' Social Security Act, §97 Civil Servants Health and Accident Insurance Law).

303. Accident treatment includes the provision of:

- medical assistance (*Ärztliche Hilfe*) in a doctor's practice;
- remedies (*Heilmittel*) and medical aids (*Heilbehelfe*) such as medication, crutches or wheelchairs; and
- institutional care (*Anstaltspflege*), for example, in a hospital or health resort.

II. Rehabilitation

304. The main objective of rehabilitation is to restore the health of employees after an industrial accident or occupational disease to such an extent that they are able to participate not only in their professional and economic but also in social life again. Consequently, rehabilitation is divided into medical, professional and social rehabilitation (§§172, 198–201a General Social Insurance Act, §§152–154 Farmers' Social Security Act, §§99a–99e Civil Servants Health and Accident Insurance Law, §§148x–249b Commercial Social Security Act).

305. Medical rehabilitation is intended to eliminate the reduction in earning capacity caused by an accident or at least to prevent a worsening of the consequences of injury or illness. In other words, medical rehabilitation is a continuation of the (acute) treatment of an accident; it provides the same services, basically medical assistance or institutional care.

306. Occupational rehabilitation involves measures designed to enable an ill employee to pursue not only his or her former but also a new occupation. This usually involves training or retraining. It is also possible to grant loans or help in finding a suitable new job (§198 General Social Insurance Act). In the case of retraining, an interim allowance (*Übergangsgeld*) is often granted as a supplementary cash benefit for the period of vocational rehabilitation (§199 General Social Insurance Act, §148z Farmers' Social Security Act). The interim allowance amounts to 60% of the calculation base and is increased for each relative of the insured person.

307. Social rehabilitation is intended to restore one's ability to participate in everyday and social life (social participation). The employee should be able to help himself again and be reintegrated into society. This benefit can also be a loan or subsidy used to adapt the apartment or car, for instance (§201 General Social Insurance Act).

III. Remedies

308. To ensure the success of the healing process and to reduce any further damage to health, the impaired employee must be provided with adequate equipment such as body replacements (e.g., prostheses, dentures), orthopaedic aids (e.g., shoe insoles or shoes with different heel heights), bandages or mobility aids (e.g., crutches or wheelchairs). This also includes their future maintenance or further adaptation according to the employee's personal circumstances (§202 General Social Insurance Act).

§3. Cash Benefits

309. Cash benefits include integrity payment (*Integritätsabgeltung*), family allowance, daily allowance, disability pension and disability allowance, as well as the various forms of survivors' pensions. The amount of the cash benefits is essentially based on the employee's previous earnings and the extent of his or her incapacity to work.

310. In principle, disability pensions are determined by the calculation base and extent of the reduction in earning capacity (§205 General Social Insurance Act). Survivors' pensions are based on the calculation base of the insured person(s) (§213 section 1 General Social Insurance Act). The calculation base for both employees and civil servants for the insurance benefit is the sum of earnings during the last calendar year prior to the occurrence of the insured event (§179 General Social Insurance Act, §93 Civil Servants Health and Accident Insurance Law); the limit is the maximum contribution base (for compulsorily insured self-employed persons, a standard value applies; *see* §181 General Social Insurance Act, §148f Farmers' Social Security Act). In the case of persons who are still undergoing vocational training at the time of the accident, that is, in particular, pupils or students, the calculation base is adjusted after they have completed their education.

I. Disability Pension and Disability Allowance

A. Disability Pension for Employees

311. The disability pension (*Versehrtenrente*) is a monthly cash benefit intended to compensate for the loss of income resulting from the reduction in earning capacity within the General Social Insurance Act and the Civil Servants Health and Accident Insurance Law (for provisions on civil servants *see* §§101 et seq. Civil Servants Health and Accident Insurance Law; designed in a different way for farmers *see* §149d Farmers' Social Security Act for more details). An employee is entitled to a disability pension if his or her earning capacity is reduced by at least 20% as a result of an accident at work or occupational disease (§203 section 1 General Social Insurance Act). The employee is entitled to a disability pension from the end of the period of sick leave caused by the accident or occupational disease, and in any case, no later than six months after the accident (§204 General Social Insurance Act). If an employee is also entitled to sickness benefit, the disability pension is paid only to the extent that it exceeds the sickness benefit (§90a General Social Insurance Act).

312. Regarding the disability pension, however, a distinction is made between a reduction in work capacity caused by an abstract occupational disease and one caused by a concrete one: in the case of a concrete occupational disease (in contrast to an abstract occupational disease), a reduction in earning capacity of at least 50% is required (§203 section 2 General Social Insurance Act).

313. In any case, the reduction in earning capacity has to last more than three months after the accident or occupational disease has occurred (§203 General Social Insurance Act).

314. The amount of the disability pension is calculated according to the calculation base and the degree of reduction in earning capacity caused by an accident at work or occupational disease. The disability pension amounts to two-thirds of the calculation base per year as long as the employee is completely incapable of work (*Vollrente*, §205 section 2 No. 1 General Social Insurance Act).

315. If the employee is only partially incapable of work, it amounts to that part of the full pension, which corresponds to the degree of reduction in earning capacity (*Teilrente*; §205 section 2 No. 2 and section 3 General Social Insurance Act). The disability pension is calculated as an annual pension but is paid out monthly (fourteen times a year, §182a General Social Insurance Act). The disability pensions are adjusted annually.

316. As regards the duration of a disability pension, it is necessary to distinguish between the permanent and the temporary disability pension: the temporary disability pension (*vorläufige Versehrtenrente*) is considered a temporary benefit for the first two years (§§209, 183 General Social Insurance Act) because, during this period, the development of the consequences of the accident at work or occupational disease is usually not yet foreseeable. In the event of improvement or worsening of the state of health, such a provisional pension can be redetermined at any time upon application or by the authorities. No later than two years after the accident or the beginning of the occupational disease, respectively, the provisional pension is converted to a permanent benefit. The permanent pension is granted until death; the entitlement exists in parallel with another pension entitlement.

317. If another accident at work or occupational disease occurs and the sum of the total reduction in earning capacity is 50% or more, a so-termed total pension (*Gesamtrente*) must be determined after two years at the latest (§210 section 1 General Social Insurance Act).

318. Disabled persons who are entitled to a disability pension of at least 50% or to several disability pensions, which together amount to at least 50% of the full pension, are considered to be seriously disabled (*schwerversehrt*). Severely disabled persons are entitled to a supplementary pension (*Zusatzrente für Schwerversehrte*) in addition to their disability pension (§§205 section 4, 205a General Social Insurance Act). The supplementary pension amounts to 20% of the disability pension if the incapacity to work is reduced by less than 70%. If the capacity to work is reduced by at least 70%, the supplementary pension is increased by 50% of the disability pension.

B. Disability Allowance for Employees

319. If the insured person is not entitled to a disability pension (e.g., in the absence of the legally required reduction in his or her capacity to work) and has no other income or entitlement to sickness benefit, he or she is entitled to a disability allowance (*Versehrtengeld*). This is a one-time benefit, which is granted in the form of a lump-sum disability benefit for up to one year (§212 General Social Insurance Act, §109 of the Civil Servants Health and Accident Insurance Law; designed in a different way for farmers, *see* §149g Farmers' Social Security Act).

C. Disability Pension for Students and Pupils

320. Pupils and students are also entitled to a disability pension or benefit in the event of an industrial accident. To qualify for a disability pension, however, the reduction in earning capacity must be at least 50% (§203 section 2 General Social Insurance Act); otherwise, they are only entitled to the disability benefit if the reduction in earning capacity is at least 20% and lasts for more than three months (§212 section 3 General Social Insurance Act).

II. Family and Daily Allowances During Treatment

321. If the employee is in institutional care because of the after-effects of an industrial accident or occupational disease, the injured person shall be entitled to additional financial benefits. Single persons receive a daily allowance; patients with relatives receive a family allowance (only implemented within the General Social Insurance Act).

322. The daily family allowance from the accident insurance amounts to 1.6% for one relative and 0.4% for each additional relative; in total, however, not more than 2.8% of one-twelfth of the annual calculation base. The family allowance can also be paid directly to the relatives (§195 General Social Insurance Act).

323. If there is no entitlement to a family allowance from the accident insurance due to the absence of family members, daily allowance amounting to 1% of one-twelfth of the annual calculation base shall be granted.

324. The employee is not entitled to family allowance or daily allowance if he continues to receive a pension from the pension insurance or more than 50% of his remuneration (continued payment of remuneration). If the employee continues to receive 50% of the full cash and non-cash remuneration, half of the family allowance or daily allowance is due.

III. Interaction with Other Benefits

325. For injured persons covered by health insurance under the General Social Insurance Act who are entitled to sickness benefit, the family allowance or daily allowance from the accident insurance does not accrue until the beginning of the twenty-seventh week following the insured event (§204 General Social Insurance Act). If the entitlement to sickness benefit or support benefit in the event of long-term illness pursuant to §104a of the Commercial Social Security Act overlaps with an entitlement to a disability pension, the disability pension shall be suspended to the amount of the entitlement to sickness benefit or support benefit if the incapacity to work results from the accident at work or the occupational disease (§90a General Social Insurance Act).

326. Recipients of a full pension for an industrial accident or occupational disease are entitled to a care allowance under accident insurance or under the provisions of the Federal Care Allowance Act (*Bundespflegegeldgesetz, see* §3 Federal Care Allowance Act). A requirement is that the constant need for nursing care due to the after-effects of the industrial accident or occupational disease exceed sixty-five hours per month for more than six months after the insured event occurred; however, the Pension Insurance Institution, not the Austrian Social Insurance for Occupational Risks, is responsible for determining and paying this benefit. Applications for care allowance must, therefore, be submitted to the Pension Insurance Institution.

IV. Integrity Payment

327. Integrity compensation (§213a General Social Insurance Act, §149m Farmers' Social Security Act) is an accident insurance benefit intended to compensate for non-material damage caused by an industrial accident or occupational disease, for example, disfigurement or mental disorders. In a way, integrity payments are equivalent to compensation for personal suffering.

328. According to §213a General Social Insurance Act, the requirements are:

- the causation of the industrial accident or occupational disease by gross negligence in failing to comply with occupational safety regulations;
- significant and permanent impairment of physical or mental integrity as a result of the insured event; and
- entitlement to a disability pension.

329. The integrity compensation is granted as a one-off benefit. The amount depends on the severity of the integrity damage. The upper limit is twice the maximum annual calculation base of the disability pension.

V. Benefits for Relatives

330. The main purpose of accident insurance benefits is to cover or at least to temper the risk of an employee's reduced capacity to work; survivors' benefits are suitable compensation for the (total) loss of alimony payments by the employee in the event of his death. Protected dependents are essentially those to whom the dead employee was obliged to pay alimony or who cannot support themselves.

A. Widow's or Widower's Pension

331. The widow's pension is generally only due to the current widow or widower. Divorced spouses are only entitled to the widow's or widower's pension if they were dependent on the insured person at the time of death. The provisions apply analogously to registered partners. The entitlement lasts until the death of the widow or widower or until she or he is remarried (for details, *see* §§215–217 General Social Insurance Act, §§112–114 Civil Servants Health and Accident Insurance Law, §§149o–149q Farmers' Social Security Act).

332. In principle, the widow's or widower's pension amounts to 20% of the deceased's calculation base. It increases if spouses are incapacitated for gainful employment themselves or older: if the widow's or widower's earning capacity is reduced by at least half or if the widow has reached the age of 60 or the widower the age of 65, the pension amounts to 40% of the calculation base. If the widow or widower remarries, his or her entitlement to a pension ceases, and a severance payment is due, which amounts to 35 times the monthly payment of the 20% pension.

333. If the widow(er) of a severely disabled person is not entitled to a widow's or widower's pension because the death of the insured person(s) was not directly caused by an industrial accident or occupational disease, a one-time allowance of 40% of the calculation base is due (*Witwenbeihilfe*, §213 General Social Insurance Act, §110 Civil Servants Health and Accident Insurance Law).

B. Orphan's Pension

334. For half-orphans, the orphan's pension (*Waisenpension*) amounts to 20% of the deceased parent's calculation and for full orphans, 30%. The pension is granted to every orphan until the age of 18; beyond that, an orphan is entitled to a pension (upon application) if the child is attending school or vocational training, studying or is in a voluntary social year (until the age of 27 at most) or if he or she is unable to work due to illness or impairment (§§218, 252 General Social Insurance Act, §115 Civil Servants Health and Accident Insurance Law, §149r Farmers' Social Security Act).

C. Pensions to Dependent Siblings or Parents

335. Dependent parents, grandparents or siblings of the deceased employee are also entitled to a survivor's pension if the deceased was paying alimony for these groups of persons (only implemented within the General Social Insurance Act); however, all these relatives together are only entitled to 20% of the calculation base and only to the extent that widows or widowers and orphans have not yet drawn the total amount of survivors' pensions (§219 General Social Insurance Act).

VI. Contribution to Funeral Costs

336. If the death of an insured person was caused by an industrial accident or occupational disease, the funeral expenses shall be reimbursed to the extent of the fifteenth part of the calculation base. The compensation is paid to the person who actually paid the funeral costs (§214 General Social Insurance Act, §111 Civil Servants Health and Accident Insurance Law, §149n Farmers' Social Security Act).

§4. Employer's Benefit: Allowance for Continued Remuneration

337. Enterprises with fewer than fifty-one or eleven employees are entitled to the so-termed 'benefit for continued payment' (*Entgeltfortzahlungszuschuss*). This is an allowance from an accident insurance agency which reimburses the employer for the continued payment they have to grant to their employees during illness (§53 General Social Insurance Act). The allowance amounts to 50% of the continued payment for six weeks per sick employee; employers with up to ten employees even receive a reimbursement of 75% of their costs for the continued payment in the case of their employees' illness. Unlike all other allowances by accident insurance, the reason for the employee's illness or accident is of no relevance and needs not to be work-related.

§5. Prevention of Occupational Disease and Industrial Accidents

338. Besides the organizing and disbursing of insurance services and benefits, the social accident insurance institutions have the legal obligation to take measures to prevent industrial accidents and occupational diseases (*Unfallverhütung* according to §185 General Social Insurance Act). These are particularly suitable as means of accident prevention (§186 General Social Insurance Act):

(1) communicating safety information;
(2) advice and training for employers and employees as well as for other persons and institutions interested in the prevention of accidents;
(3) cooperation with companies (institutions, facilities, etc.) regarding compliance with the regulations and orders intended to prevent accidents;
(4) investigation of the causes of industrial accidents and occupational diseases and their (evaluation for prevention purposes;
(5) provision of preventive care for insured persons threatened by occupational diseases (e.g., vaccination campaigns or hearing tests); and
(6) cooperation with institutions and organizations whose tasks include the transport of injured or sick persons.

339. Furthermore, accident insurance institutions are responsible for safety advice. The accident insurance institutions must set up accident prevention services and appoint expert bodies. These are entitled to enter and inspect establishments (institutions, facilities and others) and obtain all necessary information (§187 General Social Insurance Act).

§6. Administration

I. Accident Report

340. Any industrial accident resulting in death or a total or partial incapacity to work for more than three days must be reported by the employer or other persons and bodies obliged to report to the competent insurance institution within five days. Every occupational disease must be reported, in the same way as an industrial accident, within five days of the onset of the illness (§363 General Social Insurance Act).

II. Legal Nature of the Insurance Benefits

341. The person seeking benefits receives notice from the social insurance agency of whether or not benefits are granted or refused or any changes made to them. About refused claims, the insured persons have to be informed in the form of a decree (*Bescheid*) against which he or she may bring an action before the courts that decide on the matter (§367 General Social Insurance Act).

Part VII. Unemployment

342. In Austria, unemployment insurance is an important part of the government's labour market policy. Its primary aim is to prevent mass unemployment leading to economic crises and to arrange and organize reasonable employment for all people. Accordingly, the government's labour market policy does not only consist of cash benefits; it also includes job placement measures (such as bringing the company and job seekers together) as well as other actions to stimulate the market, such as promoting older employees or advising employers.

Chapter 1. Legal Framework

§1. Competent Institutions and Financing

343. Unemployment insurance is the most recent branch of the Austrian social security system; its regulations are laid down in a separate law, the Unemployment Insurance Act; nevertheless, it is closely linked to the General Social Insurance Act since unemployment insurance depends on the existence of health insurance in terms of administration and coverage.

344. The most important institution in the area of unemployment insurance and state labour market policy is the Labour Market Service (*Arbeitsmarktservice*), formerly known as the Labour Office (until 1993). With the Labour Market Service Act, the labour market administration was outsourced from the Federal Ministry of Labour, Health and Social Affairs, constituting the Labour Market Service as a service-oriented company under public law.

345. The Labour Market Service is divided into a federal organization, nine state organizations and ninety-eight regional organizations, including six branch offices. The social partners (these include representatives of the Federal Chamber of Commerce, the Federal Chamber of Labour, the Austrian Federation of Trade Unions and the Federation of Austrian Industry) are involved at all levels. At each organizational level, these social partners play a decisive role in shaping a nationwide labour market policy as well as the different work programmes of the states and in controlling the organization. Executive bodies are responsible for the performance of the tasks: at the federal level, the executive board; at the state level, the state managing director; and at the regional level, the head of the regional office. When implementing labour market policy, they are supported by offices known as branch offices.

346. Key tasks of the Labour Market Service are the placement and counselling of job seekers, granting financial support in connection with unemployment or its prevention, advising companies and promoting training as well as further education.

347. Unemployment insurance is financed by contributions from both the insured persons and employers. Its legal basis is the Labour Market Policy Financing Act.

§2. Insured Persons

348. Unemployment insurance represents a further branch of the Austrian compulsory insurance scheme (*see* General Introduction Chapter 2). The personal scope and the eligibility criteria are regulated in the Unemployment Insurance Act.

349. In the case of dependent employees, the essential criterion for being classified as insured persons is that they are covered by health insurance (§1 Abs 1 lit a and b Unemployment Insurance Act). The majority of the insured persons are employees in the sense of §4 section 2 General Social Insurance Act (*see* General Introduction Chapter 4 §1 I) and apprentices. Employees who are only marginally employed are not covered by health insurance but only by accident insurance. Therefore, employees must earn at least EUR 500.91 per month (amount applies for 2023) in order to be insured against unemployment.

350. Other insured persons are:

- free employees (*freie Dienstnehmer*; also known as quasi-employees) according to §4 section 4 General Social Insurance Act (§1 section 8 Unemployment Insurance Act; *see* General Introduction Chapter 4 §1 II);
- those apprenticed in academic professions after graduation (e.g., trainees at the court or probationary teachers, §1 section 1 lit d Unemployment Insurance Act);
- blue-collar workers based at home (*Heimarbeiter_innen*; §1 section 1 lit c Unemployment Insurance Act);
- prisoners (§66a Unemployment Insurance Act); and
- self-employed persons, but only if they declare their entry voluntarily and explicitly (for further requirements, *see* §3 Unemployment Insurance Act).

351. Excluded from unemployment insurance are, among others:

- civil servants for whom the Bridging Assistance Act provides for similar benefits modelled on the Unemployment Insurance Act; and
- persons who have reached the age of 63 (§1 section 2. lit e Unemployment Insurance Act).

Chapter 2. Provision of Work

352. The main task of the Labour Market Service is to place job seekers with companies that are looking for workers. During the first interview between the Labour Market Service and the job seeker, their personal data and the data relevant to the job placement are recorded in order to find a suitable job or apprenticeship. During this process, the possibilities and chances, as well as a strategy, for finding a job are mutually evaluated.

353. On the basis of this consultation, a contract termed 'support agreement' (*Betreuungsvereinbarung*) is concluded between the job seeker and the Labour Market Service. The agreement includes all the activities a job seeker and his or her advisor want to undertake. It is a written agreement and binding for both parties.

354. Later, free advertisements are placed in various media (such as the eJob-Room, an official platform of the Labour Market Service), which are read by many companies. Authorized companies can view the contact data (such as name, telephone number, and e-mail address); requests from other companies are forwarded to the job seeker. In the regional offices, job seekers can use self-service computers for easy job searches (referred to as *Samsomat*) as well as computers with Internet access.

355. In addition, the Labour Market Service offers, if necessary, suitable training and further education programmes as well as subsidies for taking up employment. With respect to this, a database by the Labour Market Service provides an overview of further training opportunities. Additionally, further information is available from the Career Information Centres on occupations, training and continuing education. Job seekers can take part in events and workshops and receive individual and detailed vocational and educational advice if needed.

356. In addition, unemployed benefit recipients have to contact the regional office of the Labour Market Service responsible for them individually at least once a week; this represents the control report (*Kontrollmeldung*) according to §49 Unemployment Insurance Act. Deviations from this procedure are possible either way; due to the COVID-19 measures, some of these control reports have also been converted to digital reports.

Chapter 3. Financial Unemployment Benefits

357. The main objective of the Labour Market Service and the state labour market policy in the area of unemployment insurance is the reintegration of unemployed persons into the labour market (*see also* §46 section 4 last sentence Unemployment Insurance Act). Since this cannot always be achieved in the same way, however, the Unemployment Insurance Act also provides for various cash benefits for the insured event of unemployment, which are regulated in §6 Unemployment Insurance Act, in addition to job placement, further training opportunities and advice. The most important benefits are:

- unemployment allowance (*Arbeitslosengeld*); and
- emergency assistance (*Notstandshilfe*).

358. Other services include:

- pension advances (Bevorschussung von Leistungen aus der Pensionsversicherung);
- special support (*Sonderunterstützung*);
- further training allowance (*Weiterbildungsgeld*);
- part-time education allowance (*Bildungsteilzeitgeld*); and
- partial retirement benefits (*Altersteilzeitgeld*).

359. These cash benefits pursue different goals: in some cases, they serve as a substitute for the lack of income to cover one's own living expenses and those of the unemployed person's dependents (in particular, unemployment benefit, emergency assistance and pension advances). In some cases, cash benefits are intended to provide incentives to take measures to prevent future unemployment. This is the case for further training benefits, which enable individual employees to be trained in a new area, and also for partial retirement benefits, which motivate employers to create new jobs and enable older employees to make a gradual transition into retirement.

§1. Unemployment Allowance

I. General

360. The unemployment allowance is a benefit to compensate those who have lost income due to unemployment so that people without an income can continue to earn a living for themselves and their families. The amount is, therefore, based on the previous level of remuneration; however, family benefits may be added.

361. An insured person is entitled to unemployment benefit if he or she is available to the employment agency; in other words, he or she can and may take up employment (§7 sections 2 and 3 of the Unemployment Insurance Act) and is capable of work (§8 of the Unemployment Insurance Act), willing to work (§9 of the Unemployment Insurance Act) and unemployed (§12 of the Unemployment Insurance Act). Furthermore, the job seeker must fulfil the eligibility requirements and must not have exhausted the period of entitlement. There is a formal requirement that an application for unemployment allowance should have been submitted, for which a personal visit is generally required (for details, *see* §46 section 1 of the Unemployment Insurance Act). For the duration of the COVID-19 crisis, a digital application was sufficient.

II. Requirements in Detail

362. Every insured person is entitled to an unemployment allowance if he or she is:

- unemployed;
- fit for work;
- willing to take up reasonable employment;
- available to the employment agency; and
- can demonstrate a certain minimum period of employment and has not already exhausted the maximum period of unemployment benefit.

A. Unemployed

363. Unemployed means that the job seeker's previous employment (employed or self-employed) has been terminated in accordance with labour regulations. Furthermore, the applicant must not have taken up a new occupation. There are, however, exceptions regarding employment with a remuneration below the marginal earnings threshold (§12 section 6 Unemployment Insurance Act). Similar special regulations exist for taking up self-employment during unemployment (§12 section 6 lit b Unemployment Insurance Act). In principle, unemployment does not exist if a person attends school or university at the same time because persons in training are regularly not available for the labour market; however, there is also an exception for so-termed working students, who always have a job in addition to their education (§12 section 3 lit f in connection with §12 section 4 Unemployment Insurance Act). It is important to note that participation in training or continuing education measures offered by the Labour Market Service does not change the fact that the person concerned is still to be considered unemployed.

B. Capability

364. An unemployed person is capable of work if he or she is not (permanently) incapable of work as defined by the General Social Insurance Act (§8 section 1 Unemployment Insurance Act); persons who are incapable of work cannot be placed by the Labour Market Service and, thus, receive benefits from pension insurance (*see* Part V Chapter 1). If the unemployed person is only temporarily ill, he or she is entitled to sickness allowance (§117 No. 3 General Social Insurance Act, §40, 41 section 3 Unemployment Insurance Act). In that case, the unemployment allowance is suspended for the duration the person receives a sickness allowance (§16 section 1 lit a Unemployment Insurance Act). Therefore, the total duration of unemployment benefit is not reduced.

C. Willingness

365. Willing to work means that the job seeker is ready to:

- accept reasonable employment in the sense of §4 section 2 General Social Insurance Act, arranged by the Labour Market Service;
- be retrained;
- participate in reintegration measures; and
- make all possible efforts to obtain employment on their own initiative.

366. In principle, unemployed persons cannot be assigned to any job by the government but must be given a reasonable job. If the unemployed person refuses to take an unreasonable job, he or she cannot be punished by having his or her unemployment allowance cancelled or reduced. According to §9 of the Unemployment Insurance Act, the criteria for employment being considered as reasonable are the following: the employment:

- must correspond to the physical and mental abilities of the job seeker;
- must not harm the health or morals of the unemployed person;
- may not take place in a factory affected by strike or lockout (which demonstrates the neutrality of the state towards labour disputes);
- must be adequately remunerated, which, however, only means that the collectively agreed minimum wage must be paid; the job seeker has no right to overpayments even if he received them in previous jobs; and
- must be accessible within a reasonable time, or appropriate accommodation must be provided at the new place of work. The reasonable daily travel time for the outward and return journey can be up to two hours for a full-time job.

367. Additionally, a distinction is made with regard to the reasonableness of employment as to how long the unemployed person has already been without employment and has received benefits:

- During the first 100 days, there is occupational protection (*Berufschutz*) insofar as the unemployed person cannot be referred to a job that makes future employment in the previous occupation considerably more difficult. For example, a skilled worker cannot be referred to subordinate unskilled labour during the first 100 days because such deployment is unfavourable to the further career as a skilled worker.
- During the first 120 days, there is a protection of remuneration (*Entgeltschutz*) – partly overlapping with occupational protection; during this time, employment is

only reasonable if the remuneration for the new job is at least 80% of the assessment base for unemployment allowance, in other words, 80% of the income in the job preceding the unemployment. For the rest of the time during which unemployment allowance is received, employment is only reasonable if the remuneration for the work being referred is at least 75% of the last assessment base for unemployment allowance.
- For predominantly part-time employees, additional protection of remuneration exists. If the unemployed person can prove that for at least half the duration of the assessment period, he or she was employed for less than 75% of the normal working hours, employment is only reasonable if the future remuneration reaches at least the level of the last assessment basis.

368. Explicit regulations regarding the willingness to work and the reasonableness of employment also exist in the case of a so-termed (re-)employment agreement. Such an agreement is concluded between the unemployed person and the former employer, saying that the employment relationship will be continued after a certain period of time. Such agreements can be found in companies operating on a seasonal basis, for example, in the tourism industry. Despite such an employment agreement, the unemployed person cannot refuse to be assigned a suitable job; even if it is foreseeable that he or she will be able to return to work within a certain time, it is reasonable to expect him or her to take up employment. The aim of unemployment insurance is not to organize a specific job but to place people willing to work with suitable employers.

D. Availability

369. A person who is unemployed, capable of work and willing to work is only available to the labour market if he or she can and may take up employment and has sufficient time to do so (§7 section 3 Unemployment Insurance Act). For this purpose, the unemployed person must be prepared to take up employment subject to compulsory insurance within a certain time frame. The unemployed person must, therefore, be willing and able to accept a potential job of at least twenty hours; in the case of care obligations for (handicapped) children, for instance, the readiness would only have to cover sixteen hours (§7 section 7 Unemployment Insurance Act).

370. Activities of the unemployed person, according to the Volunteer Act, but also self-employed activities that take up too much time, would prevent their willingness to do so (§7 section 5 No. 1, §12 Unemployment Insurance Act). In order for parents to fulfil the criterion of being available to the labour market while receiving childcare allowance, the child must be cared for by another suitable person or in an institution (§7 section 5 No. 2 Unemployment Insurance Act).

371. The unemployed person must be legally residing in Austria according to national residence regulations. Furthermore, he or she must be authorized to take up employment in accordance with the Foreigners Employment Act.

E. Qualifying Periods

372. In order to be entitled to receive unemployment allowance, the unemployed person must fulfil the requirement of a corresponding minimum insurance period, that is, a qualifying period (*Anwartschaft*; §14 Unemployment Insurance Act); persons who have never been in gainful employment subject to compulsory insurance can, therefore, not claim benefits from unemployment insurance, but can only receive social assistance (*see* Part X Chapter 1). The required minimum period of insurance is met if the unemployed person has been employed in Austria for a certain number of weeks within a certain time frame before becoming unemployed (reference period, *Rahmenfrist*). The number of required weeks of employment depends on various factors, such as the age of the unemployed person and the number of times the unemployment benefit is claimed.

373. In principle, an unemployed person must have been employed for a total of fifty-two weeks in the last twenty-four months before becoming unemployed in order to be eligible for unemployment allowance (long qualifying period). If the unemployed person is under 25 years of age, he or she must have been employed for a total of twenty-six weeks in the last twelve months (short qualifying period). If it is not the first time that unemployment allowance has been claimed, the unemployed persons must have been employed for only twenty-eight weeks in the last twelve months in order to be entitled to unemployment allowance. In times of crisis, the federal minister responsible can also shorten the qualifying periods for individual occupational groups by means of ministerial order (§14 section 3 Unemployment Insurance Act).

374. In principle, the periods of fully insured employment in Austria are what are relevant; however, certain other periods are also taken into account; such substitute periods include periods of military and civilian service, as well as periods of receiving childcare allowance, weekly allowance or sickness allowance. Periods of employment within the EU are generally taken into account; due to various international legal agreements, certain foreign employment and insurance periods have to be recognized as well.

375. Furthermore, there are so-termed neutral periods (§15 Unemployment Insurance Act) which extend the above-described reference period. By extending the reference period, the unemployed person can also refer to jobs that lie further in the past. Neutral periods include times during which a person works in an employment that is not subject to unemployment insurance (e.g., periods of marginal employment) or periods of training or vocational rehabilitation.

III. Maximum Duration

376. An unemployed person is entitled to the unemployment allowance for a period of twenty weeks; however, according to §18 Unemployment Insurance Act, the period of entitlement is increased if the unemployed person:

- has worked for three years in an employment subject to compulsory unemployment insurance for thirty weeks;
- has reached the age of 40 and has worked for six years within the last ten years in an employment subject to compulsory unemployment insurance for thirty-nine weeks;
- has reached the age of 50 and has worked for nine years within the last fifteen years: subject to compulsory unemployment insurance for fifty-two weeks;
- receives unemployment allowance after completion of a vocational rehabilitation measure for seventy-eight weeks; or
- has attended a training course within an outplacement scheme (*Arbeitsstiftung*): extension for a maximum of three or four years.

377. If a new claim to unemployment allowance arises after taking up an activity subject to compulsory insurance and the unemployed person has not yet used up his previous claim to unemployment allowance, there is a so-termed right of continued receipt (§19 section 1 Unemployment Insurance Act); however, the application for such continued entitlement to unemployment benefit must be made within five years after the last receipt of unemployment benefit. If the unemployed person has acquired new entitlement in the meantime, the right to the continued receipt of allowances expires (§19 section 2 Unemployment Insurance Act).

IV. Amount

378. The unemployment benefit is composed of:

- a basic amount (*Grundbetrag*);
- family supplements (*Familienzuschläge*); and
- a supplementary amount (*Ergänzungsbetrag*).

379. Since 1 July 2020, the basic amount has been calculated on the basis of monthly contribution bases (§21 section 1 Unemployment Insurance Act). These must be reported monthly by the employer(s) for their employees and are filed by the umbrella organization of social insurance institutions. If it is not possible to calculate the unemployment benefit based on monthly contribution bases, the annual contribution base will be referred to. These annual contribution bases existed until the end of 2018. According to the current legal situation, the last twelve monthly contribution bases before the so-termed correction period (*Berichtigungsfrist*) for the calculation of unemployment allowances are taken into account for the calculation of the basic amount.

380. Example: Application for unemployment allowance on 15 January 2024. The correction period covers the year preceding the payment, in this case, from 1 January 2023 to 31 December 2023; thus, only monthly contribution bases that precede 2023 are considered for unemployment allowance. In this case, with regard to the monthly contribution bases, the months from January up to and including December 2022 represent the relevant twelve months.

381. In principle, only complete months are considered for the calculation of unemployment allowance. The term 'complete months' means that there has been employment subject to unemployment insurance on each day of the calendar month. Incomplete months are only taken into account if a complete monthly contribution base is not available. Monthly contribution bases from a previous or earlier calendar year are revalued. Additional payments are taken into account by an increase of one-sixth. From the gross value of the monthly contribution base, certain social contributions and income tax are deducted, taking into account exemptions (net income). As a result, the basic amount of the unemployment allowance amounts to 55% of the net income (§21 section 3 Unemployment Insurance Act).

382. The unemployed person receives a supplementary amount (§21 Abs 4 Unemployment Insurance Act) only if the basic amount of the unemployment allowance is lower than the equalization supplement reference rate. In 2023, the equalization supplement reference rate is EUR 1,110.26 for single persons.

383. The family supplement is paid for the support of certain relatives, namely:

- children, where they receive a substantial contribution from the unemployed person and the child is entitled to family allowance (§20 Unemployment Insurance Act); this also applies to stepchildren, elective children, foster children or grandchildren; and
- spouses, life partners and registered partners of the unemployed person if this person has no or only a small income, and the unemployed person has to contribute substantially to the maintenance of this person. At the same time, there must be an entitlement to a family supplement for a minor child or a child with a disability.

384. The amount of the family allowance is EUR 0.97 per day for each person qualifying for a supplement (value for 2023; §20 section 4 Unemployment Insurance Act in connection with §262 General Social Insurance Act). The family supplement can only be granted once for each qualifying person.

385. Overall, however, specific upper limits apply:

- if the unemployed person is not entitled to family supplements, the unemployment allowance, including the supplementary allowance, may not exceed 60% of the daily net income; and
- if the unemployed person is entitled to family supplements, the unemployment benefit, including the supplementary allowance as well as the family supplements, may not exceed 80% of the daily net income.

386. If the applicant has also worked abroad, special regulations apply regarding the amount of unemployment allowance; however, first of all, there must be an entitlement to unemployment allowance based on international treaties or EU law. If a person has not been employed in Austria for at least four weeks, the previous employment abroad is decisive. The amount is based on the remuneration for a comparable job in Austria (§21 section 7 No. 2 Unemployment Insurance Act), with different regulations for cross-border commuters (§21 section 7 No. 3 Unemployment Insurance Act).

V. Sanctions

387. If the unemployed person does not accept a reasonable new job or does not participate in a training measure, the unemployed person loses his or her unemployment allowance (§10 Unemployment Insurance Act) for the duration of the refusal plus the following six weeks. If there is a further breach of duty (such as giving false information or failing to make proper efforts to obtain employment), the duration of the withdrawal is increased by another two weeks.

388. The same applies to an unemployed person who, despite being informed of the legal consequences and without having a valid reason, fails to submit a control report. In that case, he or she loses their entitlement to unemployment allowance from that day on until they claim their continued receipt of unemployment benefit (§49 section 2 Unemployment Insurance Act).

389. If the preceding employment relationship has been terminated by the employee (due to the employee's fault or voluntarily), the unemployed person cannot claim an unemployment allowance for four weeks (§11 Unemployment Insurance Act); his or her total period of entitlement, however, is not reduced.

390. If an unlawful receipt of unemployment benefit has occurred, for example, due to untrue information or withholding relevant circumstances, the recipient of unemployment benefit is obliged to repay the allowance (§25 section 1 Unemployment Insurance Act); this may be the case, for example, if an employment relationship exists which the unemployed person has not registered. If this involves illegal work or employment, even more severe sanctions are provided for: the unemployed person has to pay back the wrongly received unemployment allowance at least to the extent of four weeks. In addition, the employer who has illegally employed the unemployed person is required to make a special contribution to the unemployment insurance (for more details, *see* §25 section 2 Unemployment Insurance Act).

VI. Suspension

391. Even if there is an entitlement to unemployment benefit, in principle, there may be exceptional circumstances in which the payment of unemployment benefit does not seem appropriate. This is especially true if the unemployed person is entitled to a benefit with a similar purpose (e.g., compensation for income) or would receive other, and therefore double benefits.

392. According to §16 Unemployment Insurance Act, the receipt of unemployment benefits is to be suspended, specifically while in receipt of:

- sickness allowance;
- maternity allowance;
- nursing allowance (*Pflegekarenzgeld*);
- further training allowance (*Weiterbildungsgeld*) or part-time education allowance (*Bildungsteilzeitgeld*).

393. This also applies to:

- periods for which the unemployed person is entitled to compensation for termination or vacation.

§2. Emergency Assistance

I. General

394. Emergency assistance (*Notstandshilfe*) is a compensation benefit in the event of loss of income due to unemployment so that people without income can continue to earn a living for themselves and their families. Emergency assistance is an insurance benefit and is due when entitlement to unemployment allowance is exhausted, and the unemployed person is still without employment. If the emergency assistance does not reach a certain level, an additional receipt of social assistance is permissible (*see* Part X Chapter 1 §2).

II. Requirements

395. The criteria for receiving emergency assistance are essentially the same as those for unemployment allowance; this is because emergency assistance is designed as a follow-up benefit after unemployment allowance: The job-seeking person must be available to the Labour Market Service; that is to say, the person can and may take up employment (§7 sections 2 and 3 Unemployment Insurance Act), and he or she must be capable of work (§8 Unemployment Insurance Act), willing to work (§9 Unemployment Insurance Act) and unemployed (§12 Unemployment Insurance Act). In addition, the unemployed person must be facing severe financial hardship (§33 section 2 Unemployment Insurance Act).

396. Severe financial hardship is present if the unemployed person is no longer able to satisfy his or her basic needs (§33 section 3 Unemployment Insurance Act), in the assessment of which the entire economic situation of the unemployed person must be taken into account (§36 section 2 Unemployment Insurance Act). Income above the marginal income threshold (2023: EUR 500.91 per month) is taken into account, as is other income from renting and leasing, for instance. However, certain subsidies for further education and training are not added (for details, *see* §36 sections 3 and 4 Unemployment Insurance Act). Furthermore, if the emergency assistance does not reach a certain level, an additional receipt of social assistance is permissible.

397. In principle, recipients of emergency assistance can also receive childcare allowance at the same time. Since it is an essential prerequisite for the entitlement to emergency assistance that the unemployed person is available to the labour market without significant restrictions, they must prove that the child is being cared for appropriately, for instance, by their partner, in a kindergarten, after-school care centre or with a babysitter.

III. Duration

398. Emergency assistance can be obtained for an unlimited period of time; however, it is granted for a maximum of fifty-two weeks at a time (§35 Unemployment Insurance Act). After this period, a new application for emergency assistance must be submitted; during that process, the existence of the requirements will be re-examined.

IV. Amount

399. In general, the amount of emergency assistance depends on the unemployment benefit basic amount:

- The emergency assistance amounts to 92% of the unemployment benefit if the basic amount of the unemployment allowance is higher than the equalization supplement reference rate.
- The emergency assistance amounts to 95% of the unemployment allowance if the basic amount of the unemployment allowance is, at most, as high as the equalization supplement reference rate. If the supplementary amount is granted in addition to the basic amount of unemployment allowance, 95% of this amount is also taken into account when calculating the amount of the emergency assistance.
- In addition to emergency assistance, a family supplement is granted if the recipient of emergency assistance also has to care for certain relatives; however, the overall limits according to §21 Unemployment Insurance Act may not be exceeded.

400. When granting or extending unemployment assistance, it must also be taken into account how long unemployment allowance has already been claimed (§36 sections 5 and 6 in conjunction with §18 section 1 Unemployment Insurance Act):

- If unemployment assistance follows after receiving unemployment allowance for twenty weeks, the basic amount of emergency assistance may not be set at a

higher level than the equalization supplement reference rate (§293 section 1 lit. a lit. bb General Social Insurance Act; value for 2023: EUR 1,110.26 for single persons per month, referred to as '*allgemeiner Grundbetrag*'.
- If unemployment assistance follows after receiving unemployment allowance for thirty weeks, the basic amount of emergency assistance may not be set at a higher amount than the minimum subsistence level according to §291a section 2 No. 1 Enforcement Code (value for 2023: EUR 1,295.00 per month, referred to as '*erhöhter allgemeiner Grundbetrag*').

401. During the period from 16 March 2020 to 30 September 2020, the amount of one's emergency assistance was equal to that of the unemployment benefit (regulated by legal measures against COVID-19).

V. Sanctions

402. The sanctions for misconduct by the recipient of emergency assistance correspond to those for unemployment benefit (for more details, *see* Part VII Chapter 3 §1 V).

§3. Pension Advances

403. In some cases, unemployed persons not only meet the requirements for benefits from unemployment insurance but also those for benefits from other insurance branches. This applies, for example, to older unemployed persons who are no longer able to perform all activities. If unemployed persons have applied for an occupational disability pension or an old-age pension, they can be granted unemployment allowance or emergency unemployment assistance as interim benefits by the Labour Market Service until the decision about allocation of pension benefits is made (§23 section 1 Unemployment Insurance Act).

404. According to §23 section 2 Unemployment Insurance Act, criteria, among others, are that:

- the conditions for unemployment allowance or emergency assistance – apart from one's capacity and willingness as well as availability to work – are met; and
- given the current circumstances, the allocation of the pension benefit is to be expected.

405. The amount of an advanced payment is limited. It may exceed neither the amount of the unemployment allowance or emergency assistance nor the amount of the expected pension. If it comes to a refusal of the pension request, the advanced payment already received is to be regarded as unemployment allowance or emergency assistance. If the pension is awarded to the unemployed person, his or her claim for the pension for the duration of receiving an advanced payment is legally transferred to the federal government for the purpose of financing the labour market policy (for details, *see* §6 Unemployment Insurance Act).

§4. Special Support for Miners

406. Due to the difficult working conditions in mining, especially the high physical burden, there are also special regulations in favour of miners in the social security law. Persons who have reached the age of 52 at the time of the termination of their employment and:

– were employed in mining businesses for at least ten years before becoming unemployed; and
– carried out mining work for at least sixty months, can receive special support as a benefit from the Labour Market Service (§1 section 1 Special Support Act). This benefit is a combination of unemployment benefits and advanced pension benefits.

§5. Further Training Allowance

407. If employees want to train or further educate themselves without terminating their employment relationship, labour regulations offer the possibility of mutually agreeing on educational leave (for more details, *see* §11 of the Employment Contract Law Adaption Act). Accordingly, the employee in question is released from work for the duration of the education or training and receives no remuneration; however, according to §26 Unemployment Insurance Act, he or she may receive a further training allowance from the Labour Market Service.

408. Employees can use a total of up to twelve months within four years for this type of education or training. They can either take a whole year of educational leave or take partial educational leave; however, each part must last at least two months (§11 sections 1 and 2 Employment Contract Law Adaption Act). The training and further education can take place in Austria or abroad, including a special course with a connection to their job (foreign language or technical training classes), but also school or university degrees; the extent to which training or further education is taken up must be approximately twenty hours per week.

409. In addition to the conditions under labour law, the prerequisites for further training allowance are: that the employee was employed by the employer for at least six months immediately prior to the beginning of the educational leave without interruption, the employment was subject to compulsory unemployment insurance, and that the employee meets the qualifying period for the unemployment allowance.

410. The amount of the further training allowance corresponds to the respective unemployment benefit (in any case, at least EUR 14.53 per day).

§6. Part-Time Education Allowance

411. If only part of the employment relationship is terminated for the purpose of training or further education, meaning that the employee continues to work at least part-time (*see* §11a Employment Contract Law Adaption Act), the employee may receive a part-time education allowance, which is also paid by the Labour Market Service (§26a Unemployment Insurance Act). In its basic features, it is similar to the further training allowance.

412. The employee in question reduces his or her working hours in order to undergo training or further training; for the hours lost, he or she receives compensation in the form of a part-time education allowance as a benefit from unemployment insurance. The employee must reduce his or her normal weekly working hours by 25–50% and continue to work at least ten hours per week. The educational part-time work must last at least four months and up to a maximum of twenty-four months. The time spent on training or further education must be at least ten hours per week.

413. The part-time education allowance amounts to EUR 0.91 per day for each hour of work by which the weekly normal working hours are reduced.

§7. Partial Retirement Benefits

414. The partial retirement benefit is another benefit from unemployment insurance. In contrast to other benefits, it is applied for by the company and also paid out to the company. An employer who employs older employees who are reducing their working hours and grants them a wage compensation is entitled to partial retirement benefits (§27 section 1 Unemployment Insurance Act). For this purpose, the employer contractually agrees to part-time work for older employees. Thus, the statutory or collectively agreed normal working hours are reduced by 40–60%. The amount of the partial retirement benefit is 90% of the gross wage costs, including the corresponding employer's social security contributions; as a result, not all additional expenses are reimbursed.

415. Older employees can reduce their working hours by means of partial retirement to create a smooth transition to retirement. This form of reduction of working hours has no negative effect on the employees' pension entitlements or their entitlement to unemployment benefits because the employer continues to pay the same social security contributions as before.

416. Workers who will reach the standard pension age within at most five years are entitled to partial retirement (for details, *see* §27 section 2 Unemployment Insurance Act).

417. Further conditions are that the employee should have been employed for 780 weeks with compulsory unemployment insurance within the last twenty-five years. This period is extended by periods caring for children up to the age of 15. Furthermore, the employee must have been employed for at least three months by the company filing the application.

Part VIII. Pensions

Chapter 1. Introduction

§1. Principles and Responsibilities

418. The statutory pension insurance basically covers all persons working in Austria, excluding certain groups of self-employed persons and those whose income is below a certain negligibility threshold. People who are not subject to compulsory insurance can decide to enter into a voluntary pension insurance scheme.

419. The primary purpose of pension insurance in Austria is to compensate for loss of income that an insured person suffers due to reaching a certain age or due to a reduction in gainful employment (Part V). In addition, pension insurance compensates for loss of income of the insured persons' relatives resulting from the death of the insured person who was considered to be the family provider.

420. The pension insurance, therefore, is described as having an income and maintenance function. In addition, pension insurance funds are used to finance measures for the rehabilitation and healthcare of the insured, which is why it is also attributed to a rehabilitation and prevention function.

421. The initial intention of the legislator when introducing the pension insurance in 1906 – at first only for (higher earning) salaried employees and, from 1939, also for blue-collar workers – was to no longer expect gainful work after a certain age. Over time, the role of pension insurance has changed significantly. In addition to the traditional old-age pension, which men can claim at 65 and women at 60 (the latter rising step by step for women born after 31 December 1963 up to 65 years as well), forms of early retirement have been developed. These forms of early retirement did not serve the primary objective of pension insurance, namely, to compensate for age-related income losses, but were regarded as instruments of labour market policy. Companies have been able to renew their workforce by sending older workers into early retirement at the public's expense. Moreover, forms of early retirement did not address challenges such as retraining and further training of older staff but rather excluded this group of workers from the labour market. This is also the reason for the regular occurrence of financing problems in the pension insurance system.

422. Today, the pension scheme is based on a three-pillar pension structure to ensure sufficient financial provision in old age:

- The first pillar is the statutory pension scheme; it is implemented through mandatory statutory pension insurance.
- The second pillar is the company pension scheme; within the framework of a company pension scheme, the employer undertakes to pay into a pension fund or private insurance company by means of a collective agreement, company agreement or individual agreement. Company pension schemes are subject to labour law and regulated by the Occupational Pensions Act.
- The third pillar represents private pension provision; this is the personal pension provision of each individual concerned. Various products are offered on the financial market for this purpose.

423. In Austria, the first pillar is very dominant, while the second and third pillars are less common. This is one of the reasons why the law on severance pay was redesigned with the introduction of the Federal Act Corporate Staff and Self-Employment Provision Act ('new severance pay', *Abfertigung neu*). According to this law, the employer is obliged to pay 1.53% of the monthly gross salary into a company pension fund.

424. A characteristic feature of pension insurance in Austria is the pay-as-you-go system (*Umlageverfahren*), which is based on a contract between generations (*Generationenvertrag*). There is no contract in the legal sense but a generational consensus. The current contributions of those currently in employment are not saved or invested but are immediately used for current benefits (pensions).

425. Demographic change intensifies the existing financing problems within pension insurance. This means that more people are currently receiving benefits from the pension insurance scheme while, at the same time, fewer people are contributing to it. The contributions currently paid into the system are not sufficient to cover the running costs, which is why the federal government is forced to contribute funds.

426. In private pension insurance, the system of financing is based on the funded scheme (*Kapitaldeckungsverfahren*). This means that the paid-in amounts are saved and earn interest in the capital market in order to be paid out to the individual insured person in the insured event.

§2. Legal Sources

427. One of the most significant reforms in pension insurance law in recent years has been the Pension Reform 2003 (Budget Organisation Act 2003, *Budgetbegleitgesetz 2003*, BGBl. I Nr. 71/2003). This reform established the formula '45/65/80' in pension law. According to this formula, after 45 years of insurance, at the age of 65, insured persons are to receive a pension amounting to 80% of their average income in life. If insured persons want to prevent such income losses, they must make up for this gap with a private pension plan.

428. The Pension Harmonisation Act 2004 (*Pensionsharmonisierungsgesetz*, BGBl. I Nr. 142/2004) is also of particular importance. Previously, pension insurance law for the employed was governed by the General Social Insurance Act, for self-employed persons by the Commercial Social Security Act, for farmers and foresters by the Farmers' Social Security Act, for self-employed persons by the Liberal Professions Social Security Act and for civil servants by the Pension Act. The Pension Harmonisation Act 2004 created a uniform pension system for all working people, in other words, for the employed, the self-employed and civil servants. The regulations are laid down in the General Pensions Act; however, the provisions of the General Social Insurance Act (or Commercial Social Security Act, Farmers' Social Security Act or Liberal Professions Social Security Act) still apply unless specified otherwise. These include rules on compulsory insurance, contributions and, for example, pensions due to reduced capacity to work or the survivors' pension.

429. This profession-based organization also has an impact on the competences of each pension insurance institution. The Pension Insurance Institution (*PVA*) is responsible for dependent employees, the Social Insurance Institution of the Self-Employed (*SVS*) for self-employed persons as well as farmers and foresters, and the Insurance Institution for Public Servants, Railways and Mining (*BVAEB*) for railway workers, miners and public servants.

430. In pension insurance law, the legislator must also comply with the protection of legitimate expectations, which is derived from the principle of equality. This means that no extensive modifications of the pension law can be made applicable to insured persons who are about to retire because they can no longer prepare themselves for suddenly changed circumstances. For younger insured persons, on the other hand, extensive reductions in benefits are conceivable. In order to comply with this principle, insured persons are divided into groups to which different rules apply.

431. For individuals born before 1 January 1955, the old system of pension insurance, known as the 'old law', applies. By the year 2020, most people born before 1 January 1955 were already retired. An exception for this group of insured persons was made, where the provisions of the Corridor Pension and the Heavy Labour Pension (*see* Part VIII Chapter 4 §1 II) set out in the General Pensions Act apply. The old law is generally much more favourable to the insured than the current legal situation. In the following, the new law is being referred to unless otherwise identified, which applies to retiring people born after 31 December 1954.

432. The General Pensions Act, the so-termed 'New Law', applies to all individuals born after 31 December 1954; however, the General Pensions Act only regulates key aspects, such as the new old-age pension and pension calculation and, additionally, refers to the provisions of the old law.

§3. Overview of Insurance Claims and Benefits

433. There are three insured events in pension insurance:

(1) Age:
- (General) Old-Age Pension (*Alterspension*).
- Corridor Pension (*Korridorpension*).
- Heavy Labour Pension (*Schwerarbeitspension*).
- Special Retirement Pension (*Sonderruhegeld*).

(2) Reduced capacity to work (*see* Part V):
- Invalidity Pension (*Invaliditätspension*).
- Occupational Disability (*Berufsunfähigkeitspension*).
- Incapacity to Work Pension (*Erwerbsunfähigkeitspension*).

(3) Death:
- Widow's and Widower's Pension (*Witwen- und Witwerpension*).
- Orphan's Pension (*Waisenpension*).
- Severance Pay (*Abfindung*).

434. In addition to the pension, child allowances and, in the case of widows' and widowers' pensions, a severance payment may be paid.

435. Under the old law, and relevant to insured persons born before 1 January 1955, in addition to the Corridor Pension and the Heavy Labour Pension, there is the possibility of an early retirement pension in the case of a long insurance period or for long-term contributors. The regular old-age pension and all other pensions from insured events of reduced capacity to work and death also exist in the old law; however, the pension is calculated differently.

436. The pension insurance provides cash benefits (pensions) and benefits in kind in the event of old age, reduced capacity to work and death. Rehabilitation measures and healthcare measures are eligible as benefits in kind in certain cases. There are different types of rehabilitation measures:

- Medical rehabilitation: this includes, for example, accommodation in hospitals that are mainly used for rehabilitation, as well as follow-up curative treatment.
- Occupational rehabilitation: measures which are intended to enable the insured person to pursue his or her former or a new occupation.
- Social rehabilitation: these are measures which serve to restore the ability to help oneself and to reintegrate into social life (e.g., a loan to adapt one's apartment or to buy a car).

Chapter 2. Eligibility Criteria in General

§1. Reference Date

437. The reference date is considered to be the starting point for examining whether the insured person meets all the conditions. Potential pension entitlement is only checked at the request of the insured person (*Antragsprinzip*). Only those persons who meet all eligibility criteria on the reference date are entitled to a pension (§223 General Social Insurance Act as well as §4 section 1 General Pensions Act):

- If an application for an old-age pension or a pension due to reduced capacity to work is submitted, the reference date is the first day of the month after the application is filed (or the first day of the month if the application is filed on the first day of the month).
- If benefits for the insured event of death are applied for, the reference date is the first day of the month following the date of death (or the first day of the month if this is also the date of death).

§2. Qualifying Period and Perpetual Entitlement

438. Further conditions of entitlement include the fulfilment of the qualifying period (*Wartezeit*, §§235 et seq. General Social Insurance Act) or perpetual entitlement (*ewige Anwartschaft,* §236 section 4 General Social Insurance Act). While the qualifying period is fulfilled if a certain number of insurance months within a defined period is reached, the latter requires a certain number of insurance months over a lifetime. The qualifying period and defined period, as well as the perpetual entitlement, differ depending on the type of pension.

§3. Insurance Periods

439. In the old and new law, the concept of insurance periods is defined differently. According to the old law, insurance periods are defined as follows:

- Contribution periods: these are periods for which contributions have been paid under a compulsory or voluntary insurance scheme.
- Replacement periods: no contributions have been paid by the insured person for these periods, but the legislator has nevertheless recognized them as periods of insurance. These include, for example, periods in which maternity or sickness benefits were received; periods in which cash benefits were received under the Unemployment Insurance Act; periods of military or civilian service, and also periods spent bringing up children and bought-in periods of school or study.

440. In addition, there are also neutral periods (§234 in conjunction with §263 section 3 General Social Insurance Act) which, although they are not regarded as periods of insurance, extend, for example, the framework period for the waiting period. These include periods during which a retirement pension, a severely disabled pension or a pension due to reduced capacity to work has been drawn. Such periods may also play a role if a different type of pension is applied for later on (e.g., a retired university professor applies for a pension as a new self-employed person for her work as a writer).

441. According to the new law, however, insurance periods are defined as follows:

- Periods of compulsory insurance on the basis of gainful employment under the statutory pension insurance scheme (*Pflichtversicherung*).
- Periods of 'partial compulsory' insurance within the pension insurance (*Teilversicherungspflicht*). This includes periods during which the insured person cannot pursue any gainful employment or during which such employment is unreasonable. These situations, in which the insured person cannot pay contributions, should not have a negative impact on his future pension. For this reason, various public institutions (in particular, the Federal Government, the Federal Ministry of Defense, the Labour Market Service or a public fund such as the Family Equalization Fund) pay the contributions to the pension insurance. These include periods during which maternity or sickness benefits have been received; periods during which cash benefits have been drawn from the Unemployment Insurance Act; periods of military or civilian service, and also periods spent bringing up children. At this point, the possibility of voluntary pension splitting for child-raising periods is worth mentioning: according to §14 General Pensions Act, the working parent can have up to 50% of his or her partial credit on the pension account transferred to the pension account of the other parent for the first seven years after the birth of a child.
- Periods of voluntary insurance under the statutory pension insurance scheme.

§4. Insurance Months in Multiple Pension Insurance Schemes

442. Even if an insured person acquires insurance periods under various laws during his or her life, he or she will still only receive a pension from one insurance institution (§251a General Social Insurance Act; the principle of aggregation of insurance periods completed in different professional insurance systems, *Prinzip der Wanderversicherung*). All insurance periods are taken into account. The insurance institution for which the greater number of months of insurance has been accumulated in the last fifteen years must grant the pension. If the same number of insurance months, or no insurance months at all, have been accumulated with different pension insurance institutions in the last fifteen years, the insurance institution of the last insurance month is responsible.

443. If insurance periods with two different insurance institutions are collected at the same time, the insurance months only count as one month (*Prinzip der Mehrfachversicherung*). The legislator has standardized a certain order: the insurance month under the General Social Insurance Act counts first, then the one under the Commercial Social Security Act and finally the one under the Farmers' Social Security Act.

§5. Insurance Periods Abroad

444. For the EEA Member States and Switzerland, the Coordination Regulation 883/2004/EC applies; accordingly, insurance periods acquired in an EEA Member State or in Switzerland are treated in the same way as Austrian insurance periods for the purpose of establishing a pension entitlement.

445. According to Article 52 of Regulation 883/2004/EC, the pension insurance institution shall only calculate the amount of the benefit that would be due under the legislation it applies where the conditions for entitlement to benefits have been satisfied exclusively under national law (independent benefit). Moreover, the amount of benefit shall be determined by calculating a theoretical amount and, subsequently, a proportionate amount, also called the pro rata benefit (pro rata *temporis* method). If the independent amount is higher than the partial pension calculated according to the pro rata temporis method, the insured person is entitled to the higher independent benefit (*autonome Leistung*).

446. Many countries conclude social security agreements. In these bilateral agreements, a direct calculation method is more commonly favoured. According to these agreements, foreign insurance periods are used to assess the eligibility criteria, whereas the pension amount is calculated exclusively on the basis of Austrian insurance periods.

447. If an insured person acquires insurance periods in a country without a social security agreement, these periods do not affect the Austrian pension insurance and are not taken into account. Accordingly, an insured person who has only been employed in Austria for a short period of time may have paid into the Austrian pension system but will not receive any benefits from it.

Chapter 3. General Information on Entitlement

§1. Payment

448. The pension is paid retrospectively on the first day of the following month (§104 section 2 General Social Insurance Act). In April and October, a special pension payment is due in addition to the regular pension. Accordingly, the pension is paid out fourteen times a year. The first special payment is paid out proportionately when receipt of a pension commences (§105 General Social Insurance Act).

449. The pension insurance institution deducts a health insurance contribution of 5.1% and the wage tax from the calculated gross pension. Finally, the net pension is paid out.

450. Every year on 1 January, the pensions are automatically adjusted with an indexation factor, which follows the consumer price index and is determined annually by a regulation (§§108 et seq. General Social Insurance Act.). It is common that the legislator deviates from this form of adjustment to add a social component. Besides, from 1 January 2022 onwards, the first adjustment of a pension is made only with a certain percentage of the indexation factor, which depends on the reference date.

§2. Lapse or Suspension

451. The entitlement to a pension is suspended if the entitlement does, in fact, exist but either no benefits or only partial benefits are paid for a certain period of time:

(1) The pension is suspended in the event of imprisonment.
(2) The pension is suspended by the same amount for the duration of entitlement to sickness benefit; this applies even if entitlement to sickness benefit has been forfeited or denied; however, old-age and survivors' pensions are not suspended.
(3) The pension is also suspended if the insured person receives an earned income:
   - In the case of early retirement, the pension entitlement lapses completely if the earned income amounts to more than the marginal earnings threshold (*Geringfügigkeitsgrenze*).
   - The pension due to reduced capacity to work will be reduced to a partial pension if the pension recipient receives additional income.
   - With the normal old-age pension, on the other hand, there is no deduction in the case of gainful employment.

452. In contrast, when the pension expires, the entitlement ceases completely without further proceedings and can only be claimed once a new application has been made. The pension lapses in the following cases:

- if the person entitled (§87 General Social Insurance Act) is deceased or missing;
- expiry of time limits (§256 General Social Insurance Act; for pensions due to reduced capacity to work, *see also* Part V);
- remarriage in the case of widow's or widower's pension (§258 General Social Insurance Act); and
- the orphan's pension when the orphan reaches the age of 18 (§260 General Social Insurance Act) unless an application for extension is granted.

453. Suspension and lapse of the pension entitlement mean that the pension entitlement no longer exists; no notice needs to be issued.

454. For withdrawal of the pension, on the other hand, a formal decision is required (§99 General Social Insurance Act). The pension can be withdrawn if a benefit condition is no longer fulfilled. For example, the invalidity or occupational disability pension can be withdrawn if the pension recipient's condition has improved significantly.

Chapter 4. Insured Events and Benefits

§1. Insured Event of Old Age

I. Old-Age Pension

455. The standard insured event of old age in the pension insurance scheme provides the old-age pension; it is also called the standard pension or regular old-age pension and is regulated in §4 section 1 of the General Pensions Act. In addition, there are the Corridor Pension and the Heavy Labour Pension as special cases.

A. *Eligibility Criteria*

1. Standard Retirement Age

456. The occurrence of the insured event, that is to say, reaching the standard retirement age. Until 2023, the standard retirement age has been 65 for men and 60 for women. As early as 1990, the Austrian Constitutional Court (*Verfassungsgerichtshof*) had already declared the different standard retirement ages to be unconstitutional with respect to the principle of equality laid down in Article 7 of the Federal Constitution (*Constitutional Court 6 December 1990, G 223/88*). As a response, the legislator passed a constitutional law declaring the different retirement ages for men and women permissible until 2024, with reference to the protection of legitimate expectations (*Bundesverfassungsgesetz über unterschiedliche Altersgrenzen von männlichen und weiblichen Sozialversicherten,* BGBl. Nr. 832/1992). In addition, the legislator has introduced a step-by-step alignment: until 2033, the standard retirement age for women will be increased by six months each year starting on 1 January 2024. Thus, a uniform retirement age of 65 years will apply to all women and men born after 2 June 1968.

2. Minimum Insurance Periods

457. Fulfilment of the minimum insurance periods on the reference date (for details regarding the reference date, *see* above). In addition to the standard retirement age, for entitlement to a retirement pension, the minimum insurance period must be fulfilled by the reference date. The minimum insurance period is achieved by acquiring a certain number of insurance months. The minimum insurance period is 180 insurance months (15 insurance years), of which at least 84 (7 years) need to be acquired through gainful employment.

458. Under the old law, either 180 insurance months (15 insurance years) within a general period of 360 calendar months (30 years) or the perpetual entitlement must be fulfilled on the reference date. The perpetual entitlement is fulfilled if the insured person has 180 contribution months (15 contribution years) or 300 insurance months (25 insurance years) during his or her entire life (for the difference between contribution months and insurance months, *see* above).

459. In order to check the conditions and entitlement, the insured person must submit an application (application principle, *see* above).

460. It is irrelevant for the entitlement to an old-age pension whether the insured person is engaged in gainful employment either on the reference date or later; this does not lead to a reduction or even loss of the entitlement to an old-age pension.

B. Pension Calculation under New Law

461. The current pension insurance law aims to ensure fairness of contributions. This principle is based on the idea that the pension rate depends on the number of contributions paid during one's working life. Those who have paid a lot into the pension insurance system should receive correspondingly high pension benefits. This principle primarily benefits workers who have a flat income curve. White-collar workers often have a rising income curve. This means that they have to fall back from their standard of living when they retire unless they have contributed to a private pension scheme to make up the pension shortfall. In the old law, on the other hand, the idea of 'maintaining the standard of living' was more important; thus, the contribution amounts in the last months before their retirement were decisive.

462. One of the most significant new aspects of the Pension Harmonization Act is the pension account (*Pensionskonto*), which is used to calculate the pension benefits under the new law. The main pension association keeps a pension account for each insured person, which contains all pension insurance contributions that will directly influence one's future pension amount. These amounts are fictitious calculation values. They are fictitious because, in reality, the contributions are used directly for current benefits to other pension recipients. The pension account is held from the first month of insurance in the pension insurance scheme until the reference date for the old-age pension or death of the insured person.

463. The pension account is updated every full calendar year; for each year in which insurance periods are acquired, a partial credit is registered in the pension account. The partial credit amounts to 1.78% of the annual salary but no more than 1.78% of the annual maximum contribution base. The partial credit for the year 2023 can, therefore, be a maximum of EUR 1,457.82 (= 1.78% of the maximum contribution base of EUR 5,850.00 x 14). Income above the maximum contribution base does not increase the pension but remains free of contributions.

464. Even for periods in which the insured person does not perform any work, but public institutions make contributions on their behalf (periods of partial compulsory insurance, *see* above), 1.78% of the contributions base is credited to the pension account.

465. Part-time employees can voluntarily insure themselves (§19a General Social Insurance Act); in this case, the partial credit per month is EUR 8.92 in 2023 (= 1.78% of EUR 500.91).

466. It is worth mentioning in this context that pensions may be voluntarily split for child-raising periods (§14 General Pensions Act). Accordingly, the working parent can have up to 50% of his or her partial credit on the pension account transferred to the pension account of the other parent for a child's first seven years. The potential for pension splitting is limited to a total of fourteen partial credits. In this way, the future pension of the parent raising the child is increased at the expense of the other parent. The advantage lies, on the one hand, in fair compensation for the child-raising period and, on the other hand, in the more favourable taxation of both pensions. The application for pension splitting must be submitted at the latest when the last child reaches the age of 10.

467. A special rule applies to all persons born after 1 January 1955 who have accumulated insurance periods before and after 1 January 2005. As of 1 January 2014, an initial credit was granted to their pension account in order to cover all insurance years up to and including 2013.

468. The sum of the partial credits for the current and past years defines the total credit. To prevent an inflation-induced loss in value of partial credits from previous years, the total credit from the previous year is multiplied by a revaluation number and thus arithmetically increased (§108 section 2 in conjunction with §108a General Social Insurance Act). The revaluation number is published annually in the Federal Law Gazette and is based on the inflation rate in Austria.

469. The total credit for the last year also defines the annual pension amount when the regular old-age pension is drawn, which is paid out fourteen times a year.

470. The insured person may request a report regarding their pension account. Such a report is for information purposes only and is not legally binding. It provides information on the basis of contributions, the amounts paid, the partial credits acquired and the total credit.

C. Pension Calculation under Old Law

471. In contrast to the calculation under the new law, pension calculation under the old law is not based on a pension account system but on an assessment basis system. The formula used for this is:

> Pension amount in EUR = Total assessment basis (in EUR) x Increased amount (in %).

472. The pension amount is, therefore, determined by both the total assessment base and the increased amount.

473. The total assessment base is the total insured income during the assessment period. First, the annual contribution bases are adjusted for inflation. Then, only a certain number of the best annual bases are used to determine the total assessment base. The exact number depends on the year of the reference date. If the reference date is 2014, the best twenty-six years are used; the number increases up to 2028, the year in which the best forty years are used for the total assessment basis. Finally, the total assessment base is the monthly average of these. Accordingly, the higher the income used for the calculation, the higher the gross pension.

474. The increased amount is the sum of acquired 'increase points', which represent the insurance period. For every twelve months of insurance, 1.78% of 'increase points' are earned. For forty-five years of insurance, this results in an increase of 80%, which corresponds to the pension formula 45/65/80. The longer the period of insurance, the more 'points of increase' are achieved and the higher the gross pension.

475. At the same time, a settlement pension is also calculated by applying the legal conditions in force on 31 December 2003. Under the old law, the actual pension may not fall below a certain percentage of the settlement pension. The percentage depends on the year of the reference date. In 2023, it is 90.25%.

D. Increased Pension by Exceeding the Standard Retirement Age

476. If someone remains working beyond the standard retirement age even though they meet the minimum requirements, they will be rewarded with an increased old-age pension (§5 section 4 General Pensions Act). For each month of working after this, the pension is increased by 0.35%, up to a maximum of 12.6% (this corresponds to three further years of working). In addition, during this period, half of the pension insurance contribution of the acquired salary is paid from pension insurance funds.

E. Increased Pension Through an Additional Income

477. Termination of employment is not required for the entitlement to an old-age pension. Anyone who receives an old-age pension can, therefore, enter into an employment relationship, continue the previous one or earn income from self-employment. The pension benefit is not reduced by doing so and gains the features of an old-age bonus. For this income, pension insurance contributions must also be paid. If the additional income is above the marginal earnings threshold, it results in a special higher insurance; as a result, the regular old-age pension will be increased by a special higher insurance amount in the year after the year of employment (§248c General Social Insurance Act). For this, an annual application must be submitted.

F. Increased Pension Through an Early Start in the Working Life

478. Since 2022, if someone has worked at a young age, they will be rewarded with an increased old-age pension and an increased pension due to incapacity to work. This so-termed early starter bonus (*Frühstarterbonus*) was introduced as a replacement for the deduction-free early retirement pension for long-term contributors. To be eligible, the insured person must have accumulated a total of 300 months of contributions due to employment, and at least twelve of them must be collected before the first of the month after the person's twentieth birthday. As a result, in 2023, the monthly pension increases by EUR 1,03 per month of contribution due to employment before the first of the month after the person's twentieth birthday (with a maximum of EUR 61,86).

II. Benefits in the Case of Early Retirement

A. General

479. For insured persons who have already made many contributions to the pension insurance scheme, the insured event of old age will have already occurred before they reach the regular retirement age. In these cases, the term early retirement or early pension is used. The possibility of taking early retirement has been pushed back due to financial reasons. The following forms of early retirement exist:

- the Corridor Pension (§4 section 2 General Pensions Act); and
- the Heavy Labour Pension (§4 section 3 General Pensions Act).

480. Two reasons, in particular, make both forms of early retirement less attractive and, therefore, simultaneously promote gainful employment until the regular retirement age.

481. One is a pension deduction, according to which the pension amount is reduced for each month an early retirement pension is drawn before reaching the regular retirement age (§5 section 2 General Pensions Act).

482. In addition, a ban on gainful employment is intended to reduce the use of early retirement schemes: according to this, the insured person is no longer entitled to an early pension if he or she receives an earned income above the marginal earnings threshold (§9 section 1 General Pensions Act; in contrast to the regular old-age pension where additional income does not reduce the pension; for an exception *see* §32 General Pensions Act, according to which, during 2020 and 2021, this did not apply for persons who entered into an employment relationship regarding a healthcare profession to help overcoming the COVID-19-crisis). Only when the insured person reaches the regular retirement age, and the early retirement pension is thus automatically converted into a regular old-age pension, can unlimited additional income be earned in addition to the old-age pension.

483. In order to take advantage of any form of early retirement, the insured person must submit an application. Whether he or she does so is up to them – nobody is forced into early retirement. For older unemployed people, early retirement might be a good option from a financial point of view, as it might be higher than unemployment benefit or emergency unemployment assistance (*see* Part VII Chapter 3 §1 IV and §2 IV).

B. Corridor Pension

484. The Corridor Pension, which is regulated in §4 section 2 General Pensions Act, applies both to insured persons covered by the General Pensions Act and to those covered by the old law.

485. The Corridor Pension offers long-term contributors the opportunity to claim an old-age pension before reaching the regular pension age. To be eligible, the insured person must:

- have reached the age of 62. This age limit applies equally to men and women; however, because women can currently already receive the regular old-age pension at an earlier age, the Corridor Pension will not become relevant to them until 2027, when their statutory retirement age will have been gradually raised to 62 (and afterwards to 65); and
- have a minimum insurance period of 480 insurance months (= 40 insurance years).

486. A deduction of 0.425% is made for each month of earlier use before reaching the regular retirement age (in total, a maximum of 15.3% (0.425% x 12 months x 3 years)). In addition, a ban on gainful employment applies.

C. Heavy Labour Pension

487. Moreover, insured persons under both the General Pensions Act and the old legislation have the option of claiming a Heavy Labour Pension. The possibility of claiming a Heavy Labour Pension is available to insured persons who have done a significant amount of heavy labour in their working lives. A Heavy Labour Pension is available to those insured who:

- have reached the age of 60. For women, therefore, the Heavy Labour Pension will only become relevant from 2024 onwards, as the pension age is gradually raised; and
- have acquired at least 540 months of insurance (45 years of insurance) with at least 120 months of heavy work (10 years of heavy work) within the last 20 years before the reference date.

488. Which activities define a 'heavy work month' is determined in the Regulation of the Federal Ministry of Social Affairs, Generations and Consumer Protection on Heavy Labour (BGBl. II Nr. 104/2006).

489. A deduction of 0.15% is made for each month of earlier use before reaching the regular retirement age (in total, a maximum of 9% (0.15% × 12 months × 5 years)). In addition, a ban on gainful employment applies.

D. *Forms of Early Retirement Pensions under Old Law*

490. Insured persons under the old law are not only entitled to a Heavy Labour Pension and Corridor Pension but also to other options. These other forms of early retirement have been abolished but still apply as part of the transitional legislation (for transitional legislation, *see* §§253b, 607 sections 10–14a, 617 section 13 General Social Insurance Act and §16 section 3 General Pensions Act).

491. These include, first of all, early retirement pensions based on a long insurance period. By adjusting the minimum insurance period and the minimum retirement age, this form of retirement pension is very similar to the Corridor Pension.

492. Furthermore, the transitional law recognizes an early retirement pension for long-term contributors. The gradual increase of the minimum retirement age does not apply to certain age groups. The minimum retirement age ranges from 60 or 62 years for men and from 55 to 62 years for women, depending on the date of birth. Pension insurance contributions must have been paid for 540 months in order to take advantage of this form of early retirement pension. Colloquially, this is known as the 'Working stiff-Regulation' (*Hacklerregelung; 'Hackler'* means a person in between a working stiff and a crafter).

493. The third form of early retirement under the old law is the early retirement pension for long-term contributors who have been doing heavy labour. Only persons with an extremely long insurance history and having worked a considerable amount of heavy labour can take advantage of this. Compared to the 'Working stiff-Regulation', the 'Heavy Labour Regulation' requires a lower minimum retirement age (60 years for men and 55 years for women) and allows lower pension deductions.

E. *Special Pension*

494. Special pension benefits (*Sonderruhegeld*) are due to those insured persons who have predominantly worked night shifts and heavy labour during their professional lives. The special pension is equal in size to the disability pension (*see* above in the case of an insured event of reduced capacity to work). The minimum age for the special pension is 57 years for men and 52 years for women. In order to finance this form of early retirement pension, the employer must pay a contribution for employees who work night shifts and heavy labour on at least six working days per calendar month. This amounts to 3.80% of the general contribution base.

F. Bridging Allowance

495. The bridging allowance (*Überbrückungsgeld*) for construction workers under the Construction Workers' Leave Act and Severance Pay Act is another form of early retirement. If construction workers have reached the age of 58, they can draw their collectively agreed minimum wage for another year in the form of a bridging allowance. The requirements are that they are no longer in an employment relationship, have worked as construction workers for a certain amount of time and are entitled to an old-age pension directly after receiving the bridging allowance. The bridging allowance is financed by employer contributions and an annual payment from the pension insurance institution. It is paid by the construction workers' vacation and severance pay fund.

§2. Insured Event of Reduced Capacity to Work

496. Pensions due to the insured event of a reduced capacity or incapacity to work are covered by several branches of social insurance in Austria (*see* also Part V Chapter 2).

§3. Insured Event of Death

I. General

497. The survivor's pension is derived from the insured person's insurance claim. The pension amount, therefore, depends, among other things, on the pension the deceased member would already have been entitled to.

498. In the event of the death of the insured person, the pension insurance provides the following cash benefits:

- Widows' and widowers' pensions, including the pension for the surviving registered partners (§258 General Social Insurance Act, §136 Commercial Social Security Act, §127 Farmers' Social Security Act).
- Orphan's pension (§260 General Social Insurance Act, §138 Commercial Social Security Act, §129 Farmers' Social Security Act).
- Severance pay (§269 General Social Insurance Act, §148a Commercial Social Security Act, §139a Farmers' Social Security Act).

499. The qualifying criterion for all three insured events of death is the fulfilment of the waiting period. The same short waiting period applies as for the pension for reduced capacity to work:

- If the reference date is before the age of 50, the insured person must have acquired 60 insurance months (5 years) within a period of 120 calendar months (10 years).
- If the reference date occurs after the age of 50, the waiting period is increased stepwise to a maximum of 180 months (15 years) and the overall period to 360 months (30 years).
- The perpetual entitlement is fulfilled if the insured person has accumulated a total of 180 contribution months (15 years with a maximum of 12 self-insurance months) or 300 insurance months (25 years).

500. The reference date is the first day of the month following the death of the insured person (*see* above).

II. Widows' or Widowers' Pension

A. Eligibility Criteria

501. The surviving partner is only entitled to benefits if he or she was married to the insured person at the time of death. Whether the surviving partner was entitled to alimony at that time is irrelevant.

502. A divorced partner may also be entitled to a widow's or widower's pension; however, only if the deceased person was obliged to pay alimony to him or her, or even if she regularly paid him alimony without being legally obliged to do so. Furthermore, the surviving partner must have not yet entered into a new marriage or registered partnership.

503. The provisions for widows' and widowers' pensions also apply to registered partners as defined in the Registered Partnership Act. Unmarried partners have no entitlement.

504. The legislator wants to avoid so-termed supply marriages (*Versorgungsehen*). Such marriages are only contracted because a benefit is soon to be expected from the insured event of death. This is presumed to be the case if the marriage has remained childless and has not lasted for a long time. The length of this period depends on the age and age difference of the couple and existing pension entitlements. If this is the case, the surviving partner is only entitled to the widowers' or widow's pension for a limited period of two and a half years (§258 sections 2 and 3 General Social Insurance Act).

505. If the married couple had children, the surviving partner is entitled to a time-unlimited widow's or widower's pension. The same applies if the surviving partner is already thirty-five years old at the time of death or if the surviving partner is not 35 years old, but the marriage has lasted at least ten years.

B. Pension Amount

506. The amount of the widow's or widower's pension depends on the pension amount to which the deceased member was or would have been entitled. This shows that the widow's or widower's pension is a derived entitlement from the pension entitlement of the person insured.

507. The amount of the widow's or widower's pension ranges between 0% and 60% of the deceased's theoretical or actually paid-out pension. The percentage depends on the surviving partner's own income. The higher the surviving partner's income, the lower the widow's or widower's pension (and vice versa); in some cases, a widow's or widower's pension may not be awarded at all.

508. If the sum of the survivor's own income and their widow's or widower's pension per month does not reach a certain threshold (2023: EUR 2,220.47), the percentage of the survivor's pension must be increased until this threshold is reached (*see* §§264 sections 6 and 259 General Social Insurance Act); however, the maximum amount is 60% of the pension to which the deceased would have been entitled.

509. The sum of one's personal income and the widow's or widower's pension per month may not, however, exceed 60 times the maximum daily contribution base (*see* § 264 Abs 6a *ASVG*); therefore, a survivor's pension is not applicable if the income is correspondingly high.

510. A divorced spouse's entitlement to a widow's or widower's pension is limited to the amount of alimony formerly received. In addition, the entitlement to pension benefits ceases if the surviving partner receiving the widow's or widower's pension remarries. Because of that, widows and widowers might not marry again. To avoid this, in the event of remarriage, widows and widowers receive a severance payment amounting to 2.5 years' contributions. If the new marriage leads to divorce through no fault of the remarried widow or widower, the previous entitlement to a widow's or widower's pension is preserved. In this case, however, alimony payments from the terminated second marriage will have to be taken into account.

III. Orphan's Pension

511. Surviving children, adopted children and stepchildren of the deceased are entitled to an orphan's pension until the age of 18; beyond that age, only on special application, for example, if the child is in education or is incapable of working; however, the orphan's pension is granted at the longest until the child reaches the age of 27.

512. A half-orphan receives 40%, and a full orphan receives 60% of the full amount of the widow's or widower's pension; in other words, 40% or 60% of the pension amount of the deceased.

IV. Severance Pay

513. A severance payment (one-time cash benefit) is granted to the spouse, the registered partner and children, elective children and stepchildren only if no survivor's pension is available because the waiting period has not been completed, but at least one month of contributions has been paid.

514. A severance payment is also due if the waiting period for entitlement to a survivor's pension has been fulfilled, but there are no eligible survivors. In this case, other relatives are entitled to a severance payment, such as parents and children of full age.

V. Supplementary Benefits

A. Equalization Supplement

515. Austria, as a modern welfare state, also supports elderly people who have not been able to acquire a pension entitlement that would secure their livelihood from their gainful employment. Time spent bringing up children, part-time work or unemployment can have a negative impact on the pension level. The aim of ensuring a minimum income for all insured persons in old age is pursued by the 'equalization supplement'. In this respect, it is to be regarded as a social support benefit.

516. The general prerequisite for the insured person to be entitled to an equalization supplement is that the insured person is entitled to a pension and has his lawful, habitual residence in Austria.

517. The amount of the equalization supplement is the difference between the statutory equalization supplement reference rate and the total net income (§293 General Social Insurance Act). In 2023, the equalization supplement reference rate is EUR 1,110.26 for single persons and EUR 1,751.56 for spouses living in a joint household. If the total net income exceeds this reference rate, no equalization supplement is due. In this respect, the equalization supplement reference rate thus determines a 'minimum subsistence level' and represents a kind of poverty line.

518. The total net income includes not only the pension of the insured person but almost every additional net income. It also includes the income of a spouse living in the joint household. Net income includes, for example, income from gainful employment, alimony claims, unemployment benefit or any income from renting or leasing. Not included in the total net income are, for example, housing assistance, care allowance or child benefits.

B. Child Benefit

519. Child benefit (§252 section 2 General Social Insurance Act) is granted for pension benefits from the insured event of old age and the insured event of reduced capacity to work. The monthly payment per child is EUR 29.07. The payment is due until the child reaches the age of 18. In addition, child benefit may be granted on special application until the child reaches the age of 27.

Part IX. Handicapped Persons

520. In Austria, there are only a few specific rules or benefits for the handicapped in the field of social insurance. One reason is that social insurance requires current or previous employment. Benefits in the field of accident insurance are granted in the case that the impairment has been caused by a professional disease or a work accident; if, therefore, a handicap is the result of such an event, benefits are granted. Health insurance, however, only applies in the case of illness, which is – unlike a handicap – explicitly defined as a temporary impairment of the body or the psyche; permanent handicaps, therefore, are not covered.

521. Due to a lack of employment and proper social insurance, most handicapped persons may only refer to benefits in the field of social welfare, especially minimum income benefits and benefits for long-term care.

Part X. Minimum Income Benefits, Long-Term Care and Specific Compensation Benefits

522. Benefits of social welfare are sometimes seen as the 'last social safety net' for persons in need of support who are not entitled to other benefits. The various types of social welfare are financed by tax revenues; welfare does not operate in accordance with the insurance principle. However, it is required that the persons concerned are undergoing a financial crisis. Besides social assistance in the form of minimum income benefits in cash and in kind (*Sozialhilfe*), social welfare benefits also include benefits for long-term care (*Pflegevorsorge*). The third type of social security is that of supporting compensation benefits for specific victims and as a reward for exceptional conduct.

Chapter 1. Social Assistance

§1. Definition and Types

523. Social assistance is divided into general social assistance and the area of providing specific nursing and care. Benefits of general social assistance are, for example, monthly cash benefits to secure living costs and housing needs. In addition, the recipients of social assistance are health-insured. Examples of one-off assistance in situations of personal financial crisis are grants for funeral expenses or personal assistance to facilitate work.

§2. Criteria

524. Social assistance benefits, some of which are also called social care or minimum security, are financed through tax revenues. They do not operate in accordance with the insurance principle; beneficiaries are not required to have paid contributions. The main criterion for granting benefits is economic hardship of the recipient; in particular, that the recipient is no longer able to cover their own subsistence or housing needs by themself or with the help of their relatives.

525. Social assistance is granted as a subsidiary and individual benefit: Persons are only entitled as long as there is no coverage by social insurance or other state institutions, and the fulfilment of the prerequisites must be examined in each individual case. As a matter of principle, the potential benefit recipient must use his or her own means and efforts to earn a living.

§3. Legal Basis

526. Social assistance is covered by the outdated term 'caring for the poor' as a special competence in the Federal Constitutional Law (*see* General Introduction Chapter 3 §2 I).

Chapter 2. Long-Term Care

§1. Definition

527. Long-term care *(Pflegevorsorge)* offers assistance to people who are not (or are no longer) able to organize their lives in a self-determined manner and, therefore, require constant care and support from another person (§1 Federal Care Allowance Act). However, the need for care must be a permanent condition or last for at least six months (§4 section 1 Federal Care Allowance Act). It must be related, for example, to age or (psychological or physical) disability. If, on the other hand, it is an illness that can be treated and cured, the health insurance institution is responsible.

528. Benefits from long-term care are tax-financed by the federal government; the beneficiaries do not have to have previously paid any contributions.

§2. Criteria

529. The primary benefit of long-term care is the long-term care allowance; it is intended to provide a flat-rate compensation for additional care-related services received by the person in need of care (§1 Federal Care Allowance Act). This money is intended to enable the person in need of care to purchase the services necessary for care (such as nursing care or domestic help). Only in exceptional cases are benefits in kind granted.

530. According to §3 of the Federal Care Allowance Act, a person is entitled to care allowance:

- if he or she is in need of long-term care (at least six months); and
- he or she is also entitled to a basic benefit such as an old-age pension in accordance with the General Social Insurance Act, Farmers' Social Security Act, Commercial Social Security Act and so on, or a disability pension or rehabilitation allowance.

531. Furthermore, according to §22 of the Federal Care Allowance Act:

- The person in need of care must submit an application to the legal entity providing the above-mentioned basic benefit.
- Apart from that, the person in need of care must have his or her habitual residence in Austria or some other EEA State.

§3. Amount of Care Allowance

532. The amount of the long-term care allowance varies depending on the extent of the need for care, there being seven levels. The extent of the need for care is assessed by a doctor, expressed in the number of hours of care required per month:

Average Need for Care	*Level*	*Amount Per Month (2023)*
More than 65 hours	1	EUR 175.00
More than 95 hours	2	EUR 322.70
More than 120 hours	3	EUR 502.80
More than 160 hours	4	EUR 754.00
More than 180 hours	5	EUR 1,024.20
More than 180 hours, if:	6	EUR 1,430.20
– care measures are required that cannot be timed and have to be provided regularly during the day and night; or – the permanent presence of a carer during the day and night is necessary due to potential self-endangerment or external hazards.		
More than 180 hours if no targeted movements of the four extremities are possible	7	EUR 1,879.50

Chapter 3. Social Compensation Benefits for Victims and as a Reward

533. Social compensation, as the third part of Austrian social security, is divided into two groups: some benefits are granted as a compensation for damages to extraordinary victims of measures of the state or comparable risks, and others are granted as a reward for exceptional services to the state or the common good. Specific care benefits are financed by tax revenue; beneficiaries need not have made contributions.

534. Benefits of care for special victims are due, for example, according to:

- War Victims Care Act (*Kriegsopferversorgungsgesetz 1957, KOVG 1957*, BGBl. Nr. 152/1957), providing a pension for damage to health resulting from military service in a war.
- Prisoner of War Compensation Act (*Kriegsgefangenenentschädigungsgesetz, KGEG,* BGBl. I Nr. 142/2000) granting a compensation for prisoners of war.
- Victims' Welfare Act (*Opferfürsorgegesetz*, BGBl. Nr. 183/1947), granting benefits to persons who suffered a personal injury in the fight for a free Austria between 1933 and 1945.
- Vaccination Damage Act (*Impfschadengesetz*, BGBl. Nr. 371/1973), for damages that occurred as a result of compulsory or recommended vaccinations.
- Military Service Compensation Act (*Heeresentschädigungsgesetz, HEG*, BGBl. I Nr. 162/2015), for damages to soldiers.
- Crime Victims Act (*Verbrechensopfergesetz*, BGBl. Nr. 288/1972), for victims of a crime.
- Penitentiary System Act (*Strafvollzugsgesetz*, BGBl. Nr. 144/1969), for damages suffered by inmates during their imprisonment while carrying out work.
- Pension Act on Victims in Care Institutions (*Heimopferrentengesetz, HOG*, BGBl. I Nr. 69/2017) for victims of violence and abuse in care institutions.

535. Benefits for special services are mainly paid to officials. The classical civil servant pension is a reward for special services to the state and is regulated in the Pension Act 1965 as a form of retirement benefit. Today, however, as part of the harmonization of social security systems, the payment of pension contributions is also compulsory in this area.

Part XI. Claims and Adjudication

536. On account of their legal nature, social security benefits by the insurance bodies are granted as public law allowances. This means that – at the first level – an executive body (e.g., the Austrian Health Insurance Fund) is competent as to the decision of whether or not a denied benefit should be granted.

537. Due to the lack of more specific rules, the *Allgemeine Verwaltungsverfahrensgesetz 1991* (*AVG*, BGBl. Nr. 51/1991) is applicable. The type of legal remedy against a negative decree from the social security body depends on which kind of claim is concerned. In the case of claims to an insurance benefit, the remedy has to be brought before the courts (§367 General Social Insurance Act). This constitutes – at first sight – an exception to the principle of separation of the state powers; however, the courts do not decide on the basis of the administrative decree as such but decide the matter on their own account. Decrees on administrative affairs, such as which insurance body is competent to grant the benefit in question, have to be brought before the Federal Administrative Court.

Part XII. Modifications in General Tort Law by Social Security Law

538. The social security laws contain, under the heading 'damages and liability', special civil law regulations with regard to social security law (§§332–337 General Social Insurance Act, §§190 et seqq., Commercial Social Security Act, §§178 et seqq., Farmers' Social Security Act). The regulations combine the social insurance benefit law with the civil law compensation for damages in accordance with the Austrian Civil Code (ABGB), whereby these special regulations – due to the legal interests protected by social insurance law in general – only cover personal injuries.

539. The explicit legal link between the two areas of law is necessary because social security law regularly grants benefits regardless of who caused the damage and whether a third party could have been made (additionally) liable to pay compensation. The special regulations are thus also intended to prevent a third party who actually caused the damage from being released from liability because the social security system pays and compensates for the damage anyway. As social insurance only covers personal injury as a risk, claims from property damage do not play any role in this context; they can only ever be asserted by the injured party themselves against their employer or a third party (like a client).

Chapter 1. The Social Security Agency's Right to Recourse from the Injuring Party in the Event of Industrial Accident and Occupational Disease

540. If an employee suffers a physical injury in the course of his or her work – meaning an industrial accident or an occupational disease – or he or she even dies, the social insurance agency has to provide various kinds of benefits (e.g., medical treatment and medication). Based on an explicit legal regulation, the social insurance agency can demand compensation from the injuring third party (e.g., the employer or a client) for the social insurance benefits that have been provided if the injuring party has acted in a grossly or intentionally negligent way (§334 General Social Insurance Act). Such a recourse involves benefits from accident insurance as well as those from health or pension insurance and with regard to long-term care allowances.

541. The social insurance agency's right to recourse against the injuring party represents an original (proper) civil law claim for reimbursement of expenses by the social insurance agency; the recourse does not depend on whether the injured person is also entitled to a claim under general tort law. In other words, the public social insurance agency has its own claim under private law for reimbursement of expenses against the injuring third party.

542. Since the social insurance agency has an original claim against the injurer, any contributory negligence of the injured employee would not mitigate the recourse (§334 section 3 General Social Insurance Act). On the other hand, the social insurance agency can waive recourse against the injuring party, in whole or in part, on the condition that the harm was not done intentionally and the injurer's economic situation is critical.

Chapter 2. Employer's Liability Privilege in the Case of Industrial Accidents and Occupational Diseases

543. If an employee suffers injury due to an industrial accident or occupational disease, or if he or she even dies due to such cause, social security laws provide for a substantial reduction of the employer's liability, which is called employer's liability privilege (*Dienstgeberhaftungsprivileg*): the employer is only obliged to compensate the injured employee for damages if the employer has caused the employee's injury or death intentionally (§333 section 1 General Social Insurance Act). In all other cases (gross or slight negligence), social insurance will cover the damage; in this respect, it is a discharge of the employer's liability.

544. The reason for the explicit liability reduction is primarily the fact that only employers finance accident insurance with their contributions. Another objective of the introduction of liability reduction was to preserve the peace within a company and to avoid civil law disputes between company owner and employee; furthermore, the assertion of claims against the social insurance agency is, from a financial point of view, less burdensome for the employee than civil proceedings before the ordinary courts directly against the employer.

545. A disadvantage for the employee, however, is that the liability privilege limits the employee's claim to the extent that the employee does not have the same claims against the social insurance agency that he or she could assert against the employer on the basis of the tort law. As a result, an employee would not be granted those compensation payments which are not covered by equivalent social security benefits. This applies, in particular, to compensation for immaterial damages, such as pain and suffering compensation, which previously had no equivalent in social security law; with integrity compensation, laid down in §213a General Social Insurance Act, only a partial compensation by social security was created.

546. Social Security law extends the employer's exemption from liability. According to §333 section 4 General Social Insurance Act, the following groups also enjoy this privilege:

- the employer's legal or authorized representatives; and
- the so-termed overseer (*Aufseher_in*) in the company.

547. These groups of liability towards the injured employee only apply in the case of intentional damage. Examples of legal or authorized representatives are CEOs, directors and some legal persons. More difficult to explain is the term 'overseer' in the company, a very old-fashioned term. According to case law, an overseer does not need a formal, permanent senior position or to receive a corresponding salary. Instead, the actual output of instructions or even short-term senior authority to the injured party would be sufficient.

548. An overseer, therefore:

- is responsible for the interaction of personal and technical forces;
- must have personal responsibility for the supervision of at least one operational process;
- must be in charge of the work process (work step) at the time of the accident.

549. Practical examples include even the authority of a forklift driver unloading a truck trailer vis-à-vis his or her colleagues assisting as required.

550. (Equal-ranking) work colleagues, on the other hand, do not fulfil the concept of overseer or authorized representative; co-workers, therefore, cannot enjoy the employer liability privilege and are liable vis-à-vis their injured colleagues in accordance with civil law principles. In this case, however, the law at least restricts the social insurance agency's recourse (§332 section 5 General Social Insurance Act); as a result, the social insurance agency provides benefits to the injured employee and only has recourse against injuring colleagues acting with gross negligence or with intent.

Chapter 3. *Ex Lege* Transfer of Claims for Compensation from Injured Employee to Social Insurance Agency

551. Generally, anyone suffering physical damage through an accident can claim compensation for damage directly from the injurer. If the injured party has already received benefits from social insurance, the claim for compensation, in certain constellations, is transferred by law to the social insurance agency (§332 General Social Insurance Act). Due to this transfer of claim, the social insurance agency is entitled to demand compensation for this damage from the injurer by way of recourse instead of from the injured party themself.

§1. Extent of Transfer of Claims

552. The claim for damages against an injuring party is transferred to the social insurance agency only to the extent that the injured party receives benefits from the social insurance. The injured party can still assert claims for further damages or damages for which no social insurance benefits are due. In order to make this distinction, the claim for damages is compared to the benefits from social insurance in accordance with material, temporal and personal criteria. Social insurance benefits must, therefore, cover the same damage for the same period and be granted to the injured party (congruence). If the damage is higher than the benefits from social insurance, for example, because the insured person has to pay a deductible, he or she can claim it independently.

553. If the injured employee is contributorily negligent, the injurer, in general, must compensate the employee only for a part of the damage. This percentage, however, is not deducted in an aliquot way from the claim of the social security agency and the injured party. The claim for damages or compensation passes over to the social insurance agency without any reduction up to the amount in which it has provided benefits. The share for contributory negligence is deducted in full from the amount the injured party receives him- or herself.

§2. Assertion

554. The social insurance agency can assert the claim which has been transferred to it by law in its own name directly against the injuring party.

§3. Exceptions and Limitations

555. If the injuring party is the employer of the injured party (or their representative or an overseer), then he or she is not liable to the injured party for the damages caused (employer liability privilege). There is, therefore, no claim that could be transferred to the social insurance agency (*see* above).

556. If the injurer is a co-worker of the injured party, meaning someone who is employed in the same company as the injured party, the recourse is limited. The social insurance agency may only assert the claim transferred if the damage was caused at least by gross negligence. Exceptionally, a colleague is liable even if he or she has acted only slightly negligently when the damage was caused by a means of transport, for it is subject to a stricter legal liability. In this context, school colleagues are on an equal basis with co-workers.

557. Case law has also held that there is no recourse by the social insurance agency against family members. The reason for this is that compensation to the social insurance agency would reduce family income and would oppose the idea of insuring against risks.

Selected Bibliography

Brodil, W./Windisch-Graetz, M., Sozialrecht in Grundzügen, 9th edition (2021).
Burger, F./Mair, A./Wachter, G., Sozialrecht Basics, 6th edition (2022).
Mosler, R./Müller, R./Pfeil, W., Der SV-Komm (Loseblatt).
Pfeil, W./Auer-Mayer, S., Österreichisches Sozialrecht, 13th edition (2021).
Resch, R., Sozialrecht, 9th edition (2023).
Tomandl, T., Grundriss des österreichischen Sozialrechts, 7th edition (2019).
Tomandl, T./Felten, E. (eds), System des österreichischen Sozialversicherungsrechts (Loseblatt).

Journals

Das Recht der Arbeit (DRdA).
Journal für Arbeitsrecht und Sozialrecht (JAS).
Soziale Sicherheit (SozSi).
Zeitschrift für Arbeitsrecht und Sozialrecht (ZAS).
Zeitschrift für Europäisches Sozial- und Arbeitsrecht (ZESAR).
Zukunftsvorsorge aktuell (zuvo).

Articles on social security can also be found in the following journals

Ecolex.
Juristische Blätter (JBl).
Österreichische Juristen-Zeitung (ÖJZ).
Österreichische Zeitschrift für Pflegerecht (ÖZP).
Recht der Wirtschaft (RdW).
Versicherungsrundschau (VersRdSch).
wirtschaftsrechtliche blätter (wbl).

Selected Bibliography

List of Statutes

Act on Measures against COVID-19 = *COVID-19-Maßnahmengesetz (COVID-19-MG)* BGBl. I Nr. 12/2020 idF BGBl. I Nr. 103/2022

Act on Safeguarding Employees' Claims in the Event of the Employer's Insolvency = *Insolvenz-Entgeltsicherungsgesetz (IESG)* BGBl. Nr. 324/1977 idF BGBl. I Nr. 185/2022

Annex 1 to the General Social Insurance Act = *Anlage 1 zum Allgemeinen Sozialversicherungsgesetz (ASVG)* BGBl. Nr. 189/1955 idF BGBl. I Nr. 110/2023

Artists' Social Insurance Fund Act = *Künstler-Sozialversicherungsfondsgesetz (K-SVFG)* BGBl. I Nr. 131/2000 idF BGBl. I Nr. 112/2023

Bridging Assistance Act = *Überbrückungshilfengesetz (ÜHG)* BGBl. Nr. 174/1963 idF BGBl. I Nr. 153/2020

Budget Organisation Act 2003 = *Budgetbegleitgesetz 2003* BGBl. I Nr. 71/2003

Childcare Allowance Act = *Kinderbetreuungsgeldgesetz (KBGG)* BGBl. I Nr. 103/2001 idF BGBl. I Nr. 115/2023

Civil Servants Health and Accident Insurance Act = *Beamten-Kranken- und Unfallversicherungsgesetz (B-KUVG)* BGBl. Nr. 200/1967 idF BGBl. I Nr. 69/2023

Commercial Social Security Act = *Gewerblichen Sozialversicherungsgesetz (GSVG)* BGBl. Nr. 560/1978 idF BGBl. I Nr. 101/2023

Compensation for Family Expenses Act = *Familienlastenausgleichsgesetz 1967 (FLAG 1967)* BGBl. Nr. 376/1967 idF BGBl. I Nr. 82/2023

Construction Workers' Leave Act and Severance Pay Act = *Bauarbeiter-Urlaubs- und Abfertigungsgesetz (BUAG)* BGBl. Nr. 414/1972 idF BGBl. I Nr. 73/2022

Crime Victims Act = *Verbrechensopfergesetz (VOG)* BGBl. Nr. 288/1972 idF BGBl. I Nr. 215/2022

Employer Levy Act = *Dienstgeberabgabegesetz (DAG)* BGBl. I Nr. 28/2003 idF BGBl. I Nr. 100/2018

Employment Contract Law Adaption Act = *Arbeitsvertragsrechts-Anpassungsgesetz (AVRAG)* BGBl. Nr. 459/1993 idF BGBl. I Nr. 115/2023

Enforcement Code = *Exekutionsordnung (EO)* RGBl. Nr. 79/1896 idF BGBl. I Nr. 77/2023

Farmers' Social Security Act = *Bauern-Sozialversicherungsgesetz (BSVG)* BGBl. Nr. 559/1978 idF BGBl. I Nr. 69/2023

Federal Act Corporate Staff and Self-Employment Provision Act = *Betriebliches Mitarbeiter- und Selbständigenvorsorgegesetz (BMSVG)* BGBl. I Nr. 100/2002 idF BGBl. I Nr. 199/2021

List of Statutes

Federal Care Allowance Act = *Bundespflegegeldgesetz (BPGG)* BGBl. Nr. 110/1993 idF BGBl. I Nr. 109/2023

Federal Constitutional Law = *Bundesverfassungsgesetz (B-VG)* BGBl. Nr. 1/1930 idF BGBl. I Nr. 222/2022

Federal Constitutional Law on Different Age Limits for Male and Female Social Security Recipients = *Bundesverfassungsgesetz über unterschiedliche Altersgrenzen von männlichen und weiblichen Sozialversicherten* BGBl. Nr. 832/1992

Federal Social Assistance Basic Law = *Sozialhilfe-Grundsatzgesetz* BGBl. I Nr. 41/2019 idF BGBl. I Nr. 45/2023

Foreigners Employment Act = *Ausländerbeschäftigungsgesetz (AuslBG)* BGBl. Nr. 218/1975 idF BGBl. I Nr. 84/2023

General Administrative Procedures Act = *Allgemeines Verwaltungsverfahrensgesetz 1991 (AVG)* BGBl. Nr. 51/1991 idF BGBl. I Nr. 88/2023

General Pensions Act = *Allgemeines Pensionsgesetz (APG)* BGBl. I Nr. 142/2004 idF BGBl. I Nr. 36/2023

General Social Insurance Act = *Allgemeines Sozialversicherungsgesetz (ASVG)* BGBl. Nr. 189/1955 idF BGBl. I Nr. 110/2023

Labour Market Policy Financing Act = *Arbeitsmarktpolitik-Finanzierungsgesetz (AMPFG)* BGBl. Nr. 315/1994 idF BGBl. I Nr. 185/2022

Labour Market Service Act = *Arbeitsmarktservicegesetz (AMSG)* BGBl. Nr. 313/1994 idF BGBl. I Nr. 61/2023

Liberal Professions Social Security Act = *Freiberuflichen-Sozialversicherungsgesetz (FSVG)* BGBl. Nr. 624/1978 idF BGBl. I Nr. 110/2023

Military Service Compensation Act = *Heeresentschädigungsgesetz (HEG)* BGBl. I Nr. 162/2015 idF BGBl. I Nr. 100/2018

Notary Insurance Law = *Notarversorgungsgesetz (NVG 2020)* BGBl. I Nr. 128/2020 idF BGBl. I Nr. 209/2021

Occupational Pensions Act = *Betriebspensionsgesetz (BPG)* BGBl. Nr. 282/1990 idF BGBl. I Nr. 100/2018

Penitentiary System Act = *Strafvollzugsgesetz (StVG)* BGBl. Nr. 144/1969 idF BGBl. I Nr. 223/2022

Pension Act = *Pensionsgesetz 1965 (PG 1965)* BGBl. Nr. 340/1965 idF BGBl. I Nr. 36/2023

Pension Act on Victims in Care Institutions = *Heimopferrentengesetz (HOG)* BGBl. I Nr. 69/2017 idF BGBl. I Nr. 12/2023

Pension Harmonisation Act 2004 = *Pensionsharmonisierungsgesetz* BGBl. I Nr. 142/2004

Prisoner of War Compensation Act = *Kriegsgefangenenentschädigungsgesetz (KGEG)* BGBl. I Nr. 142/2000 idF BGBl. I Nr. 100/2018

Registered Partnership Act = *Eingetragene Partnerschaft-Gesetz (EPG)* BGBl. I Nr. 135/2009 idF BGBl. I Nr. 86/2021

Regulation of the Federal Ministry of Social Affairs, Generations and Consumer Protection on Heavy Labour = *Schwerarbeitsverordnung* BGBl. II Nr. 104/2006 idF BGBl. II Nr. 413/2019

Special Support Act = *Sonderunterstützungsgesetz (SUG)* BGBl. Nr. 642/1973 idF BGBl. I Nr. 158/2021

Unemployment Insurance Act = *Arbeitslosenversicherungsgesetz 1977 (AlVG)* BGBl. Nr. 609/1977 idF BGBl. I Nr. 118/2023
Vaccination Damage Act = *Impfschadengesetz* BGBl. Nr. 371/1973 idF BGBl. I Nr. 215/2022
Victims' Welfare Act = *Opferfürsorgegesetz* BGBl. Nr. 183/1947 idF BGBl. I Nr. 215/2022
Vocational Training Act = *Berufsausbildungsgesetz (BAG)* BGBl. Nr. 142/1969 idF BGBl. I Nr. 62/2023
Volunteer Act = *Freiwilligengesetz (FreiwG)* BGBl. I Nr. 17/2012 idF BGBl. I Nr. 105/2023
War Victims Care Act = *Kriegsopferversorgungsgesetz 1957 (KOVG 1957)* BGBl. Nr. 152/1957 idF BGBl. I Nr. 215/2022
Workers' Accident Insurance Act = *Arbeiterunfallversicherungsgesetz* RGBl. Nr. 1/1888
Workers' Health Insurance Act = *Arbeiterkrankenversicherungsgesetz* RGBl. Nr. 33/1888

www.ingramcontent.com/pod-product-compliance
Lightning Source LLC
Chambersburg PA
CBHW071343230926
51846CB00002B/431
9789403549279